Seville's
New Normal

INSIDER TIPS FOR VISITORS

2022

SECOND EDITION / SPRING 2022

Karen McCann

CAFÉ
SOCIETY
PRESS

ALSO BY KAREN MCCANN

MEMOIRS

Dancing in the Fountain: *How to Enjoy Living Abroad*

Adventures of a Railway Nomad: *How Our Journeys Guide Us Home*

TRAVEL & EXPAT GUIDES

Pack Light: *Quick & Easy Tips for Traveling Everywhere With Just the Right Stuff*

How to Enjoy Moving Abroad: *Three-Book Set of Insider Tips for Living Well Overseas*

How to Meet People on the Road: *A Guide to Forming Friendships in Foreign Lands*

101 Ways to Enjoy Living Abroad: *Essential Tips for Easing the Transition to Expat Life*

Published by Café Society Press
Clearstead
E, 1100 Superior Ave, Suite 700, Cleveland, OH 44114 USA
enjoylivingabroad.com

ISBN: 9798773081463

ABOUT KAREN MCCANN'S WRITING

"I must have laughed out loud at least once in every chapter."

Lonely Planet

"Warm, inviting, immediately charming, and constantly entertaining."

Chris Brady, author of *A Month of Italy*

"McCann's wacky sense of humor will have you laughing on every page."

Rita Golden Gelman, author of *Tales of a Female Nomad*

"Witty, fresh and engaging."

Victoria Twead, author of *Chickens Mules & Two Old Fools*

"A very dry sense of humor and a road wisdom earned from volunteering in hot spots around the world."

John Gill, author of *Andalucía, a Cultural History*

"Hilarious, inspiring, and beautifully written."

George Mahood, author of *Free Country*

"Warmth, wisdom, and humor."

Susan Pohlman, author of *Halfway to Each Other*

For my amigos and readers, whose wisdom, kindness, and laughter kept me (more or less) sane over the past two years.

And for Rich. Thanks for a lifetime of adventure.

CONTENTS

1.
HOW HAVE THE LAST TWO YEARS RESHAPED SEVILLE?

People keep asking anxiously how much Seville has changed in the past two years, and I tell them not to worry. The city is still as warm-hearted and quirky as ever and certainly hasn't lost its two-thousand-year-old capacity for charming the socks off people. Yes, I know, technically people didn't wear socks two thousand years ago, but somehow "charming the togas" off people didn't sound quite right either.

Of course, like most places on the planet, the city has seen its share of changes lately, and as an American travel writer living in Seville, I find my email inbox flooded with requests for information about this city's new normal. I often hear from folks who fell in love with the city when they visited thirty years ago, or thirteen, or three, and now they're hesitant about returning because they're worried that the city might have lost its magic.

It hasn't.

Seville is as vibrant and offbeat as ever, and those lucky enough to call this city home still have an impressive knack for enjoying life, even under pandemic conditions. The outdoor cafés remain bright with sunshine and laughter, and an atmosphere of optimism prevails. Andalucía, as southern Spain is properly known, is the most heavily vaccinated region in Spain (possibly Europe) and its Covid rate is the lowest in the nation. Overall, Western Europe is showing so much improvement that Hans Kluge, the World Health Organization's Europe Director, said recently, "It's plausible that the region is moving towards a kind of pandemic endgame … I am hopeful we can end the emergency phase in 2022."

Of course, as anyone who's ever watched a horror movie knows, making a statement like that is simply taunting fate to jump roaring out of the closet to prove you wrong. Yes, the numbers are coming down in Spain and many other countries. But a lifetime of movie-going has taught me not to count my chickens before the final credits roll. Even if the emergency phase does begin winding down this year, Covid isn't likely to disappear quietly or permanently. There will be more surprises. Life as we know it will change, again and again. So what can we do? Perhaps philosopher Alan Watts said it best: "The only way to make sense out of change is to plunge into it, move with it, and join the dance." And if there's anything Seville knows about, it's dancing. (But more about flamenco later.)

Given the uncertainty of our times, it's not surprising that friends, family, my readers, and even total strangers are writing to ask whether I think they should finally reschedule their long-postponed trip to Seville; they want to know how the city has changed and whether it's safe. In a normal year (remember those?) two million people visited Seville, and sometimes it seems as if all of them are dropping me a quick email with these kinds of questions. When it became clear I wasn't going to be able to get around to everyone individually, I decided to collect all my advice into this little guide and get it out there for all to read.

I first published this guide in late 2021, and already a lot has changed (yes, Omicron, I'm thinking of you) causing unexpected shifts in laws, policies, and social norms. So I'm publishing this second edition in spring of 2022 to include new information and additional resources you may find helpful.

"Yes, OK, fine," people keep saying. "But just tell me this: is Seville safe?"

"Compared to what?" I always ask.

Safety is a moving target these days, and no one can say with absolute certainty whether it's the right time for you or anyone else to visit Seville. But if you do decide to come, you'll enjoy it a lot more after reading this guide. Here you'll find a wealth of practical information, useful insights, and loony stories about living in Seville for the better part of two decades and through much of the pandemic.

This is not a conventional guide, with exhaustive listings of monument visiting hours, railway timetables, and hotels in your price range; you can easily find all that online. What I thought you'd really want to know is how to experience the city like someone who lives here. So I'm not going to give you a list of every flamenco *tablao* in town, I'll simply tell you where I go for electrifying flamenco shows — and where I find the best fresh *churros* (fried dough), can't-miss photos of the Three Kings parade, and a thousand other pleasures that are hallmarks of Sevillano life. This is my personal introduction to the city, the insider tips I'd share with my sisters if we were sitting up late over a bottle of wine discussing their plans to visit Seville this year.

What's the first thing I would tell them? To brace themselves for the shock of being in a city that feels almost (dare I say it?) normal. People are matter-of-fact about observing all the appropriate public safety protocols while moving on with their lives. Nobody complains about face masks, which are no longer mandatory outdoors but must be worn inside public spaces.

Many other parts of Spain have more restrictions, such as curfews, early closing hours for bars, and limits on the number of people who can gather, even in private homes. This turned out to be very bad news for a group of Americans who decided to hold an orgy in a Barcelona suburb on New Year's Eve. More than 50 participants were arrested when police raided the party — not because anybody cared about their sexual hijinks, but because they'd violated Covid restrictions limiting indoor gatherings to ten people. A neighbor raised the alarm when a couple knocked on his door by mistake and announced they were there to join the love-in. Oops!

It's not easy for any of us to cope with the stress of a world lurching from one catastrophe to another. However, blowing off steam in a sex orgy doesn't seem like a very practical solution to me. For a start, was anybody checking at the door to make sure everyone was vaxxed and boosted? And imagine the awkwardness of having to explain to the contact tracers that you caught Covid (and heaven knows what else) during a night of debauchery with multiple party animals whose names you may not know. Here in Seville, I've never heard about any orgies taking place; if they are, I'm obviously not on the invitation list. But even without that kind of high-risk excitement, you can have a lot of fun in this city.

To get you started, I'll provide guidelines for finding your way around the maze-like streets of Seville's *centro*, demonstrate why eating five meals a day and taking siestas helps you stay fit, and fill you in on the colorful backstories of the festivals that are (finally!) scheduled to come back in their full splendor this year. You'll learn about some of my favorite places to eat, including funky old family-run tapas bars and the splashy new foodie palaces that are making headlines in the culinary world. After reading this short guide, you'll know how to have fun, stay safe, and experience the city like a local — or at least, like an expat who has lived here for decades.

If you're considering heading to Seville, you can find even more information and regular updates on my blog, EnjoyLivingAbroad.com, along with photos and videos of places, events, and activities covered in this guide. My blog's comments section has become an ongoing conversation with my readers, an exchange of ideas and inspirations as well as information. I hope you'll join in.

Back in the days when global travel was more practical, I also wrote (on my blog and in my books) about the journeys my husband and I took, usually by train, often lasting many months. Rich and I explored remote corners of Eastern Europe, learned how to cook Mediterranean comfort food in thirteen nations, conducted luggage-free travel experiments in France, Kosovo, and California, and enjoyed many other grand adventures. I hope that someday we can once again roam that freely across borders.

Right now, I'm just grateful to be in Seville. Rich and I were here when the pandemic hit, and two months later we returned to the US for what we thought would be a short stay. It took us sixteen months to make our way back here. Ever since we arrived in September of 2021, I've had the pleasure of exploring the city anew, often with the same jaw-dropping surprise and heart-lifting joy — and occasional aghast moments — I feel in strange lands. No matter how many countries I've visited and how often I've stepped off a train into an unknown city, I always feel like Dorothy falling into Oz and striding onto that yellow brick road in giddy anticipation of astonishing adventures just ahead. That's how I'm feeling about Seville these days, and I hope you will too.

2.
WHEN IS THE IDEAL TIME TO VISIT?

When people ask me when they should come to Seville, I know they're expecting advice on the weather and how to beat high-season price hikes. But Seville operates on its own timetable, driven by a cycle of city-wide festivals, and your biggest decision is which one(s) you want to experience — or avoid.

In 2020 the festivals were put on hold, which was a huge blow to morale, and in 2021 the few that took place were mere shadows of their usual splendor. In 2022 they are all expected to come roaring back, bigger than ever, and pent-up desire to celebrate is likely to make the usual massive crowds swell to insane proportions. I love the heady excitement of the big spring festivals, but they are not for the faint of heart or anyone given to agoraphobia.

But all that happens later. The early part of the year is much slower and more relaxed.

Seville in winter

The city is relatively quiet from the time the year-end holidays finish up until mid-March, and for many that's the best time to get to know the city. Twenty years ago, Rich and I started visiting every February, staying longer and longer each time. We were thrilled to escape the snow belt of Cleveland, a city that gets just 69 days of full sun a year, not one of which occurs between New Year's and Easter. Abandoning our snow shovels and ice scrapers with pleasure, we'd install ourselves at Seville's sidewalk tables, sipping espresso and watching the world go by. One of the beauties of this climate is that the mild winters — a trifle too cool for serious sunbathing, entirely too warm to produce any snow for sports — offer the kind of unremarkable weather that doesn't demand excessive activity from anyone.

Except on the occasional days of rain, in winter sidewalk cafés are filed with Sevillanos doing what they do best: enjoying themselves. People in this city devote the same energy and attention to their social lives that Americans expend on their careers. Spending time with family and friends isn't something you fit in around your work schedule, it's a top priority every day and doubly so on Sundays. Here it's a tradition to have lunch with your entire family every Sunday, all year long. As you can imagine, Americans who marry into Spanish families often find this custom a trifle daunting.

Whenever Sevillanos gather, sooner or later they will talk about the two big spring festivals. These mark the transition from the shortest, darkest days of winter to the full blossoming of summer, from the dying of the old year to the coming of age of another generation of children. And they are an opportunity to party on a grand scale. For the biggest festivals, the entire city shuts down or goes on reduced hours. This is maddening for visitors who want to visit monuments and museums, go shopping, or simply get the feel of the city's daily life. But unlike some cities, which have become a Disneyland version of themselves catering entirely to the preferences of tourists, Seville holds firmly to the old ways.

Spring festivals

It all begins in the week before Easter, a liturgical holiday whose date varies every year. In Western Christianity it's calculated using the Gregorian calendar and an arcane formula involving the 19-year Metonic cycle (a lunirsolar calendar based on the work of Meton of Athens in the 5th century BCE), the March equinox, a Sunday, and heaven only knows what else. In 2022 Easter falls on April 17, so the run-up, known as *Semana Santa* (Holy Week) begins April 10. While it's a solemn religious tradition observed in the strictest form, *Semana Santa* also has its social side, with family parties and private celebrations throughout the week.

Semana Santa revolves around 54 processions, each organized by a *cofradia* (brotherhood) whose members transport statues of the suffering Jesus and weeping Mary from the home church to the cathedral and back again. The route is circuitous, carefully choreographed, and long enough to require 8 to 12 hours of marching. The statues are magnificent, often centuries old and attired is spectacular velvet robes embroidered in real gold. Their entourage generally includes at least one marching band and up to 2500 robed Nazarenos carrying six-foot candles. The Nazarenos are Sevillanos dressed as penitents in long robes and tall conical hats with draperies that cover their faces, leaving mere slits to see through. The look is anonymous, creepy, and said to have inspired the outfits of America's Ku Klux Klan. Even now, I find the sight of them distinctly unnerving.

Typically each *paso* (platform) weighs about 5,300 pounds and is carried by 40 stalwart men known as *costaleros*, each of whom bears 130 pounds of weight on his neck. I can't help but wince when I watch them hoist their burden, particularly when they add special flourishes, such as making the platform sway in a sort of dance or dropping down on their knees to pass through a church doorway. Teams of *costaleros* rotate with relief crews, and those coming off duty usually head to the nearest bar, where they are given instant service and free beer. They've earned it.

Seville's next city-wide party, the *Feria de Abril* (April Fair), is traditionally held two weeks after Easter, which falls so late in 2022 that the April Fair will take place May 1 to 7. If you're going to be in Seville during the *Feria*, pack a fancy party outfit, take a stroll through the fairgrounds, and prepare to be dazzled.

What began as a livestock fair in 1846 soon became an excuse to put up tents, dress in flamboyant clothes, and dance all night. By now there's a special fairground across the Guadalquivir River where you'll find an enormous lighted portal and more than 1000 tents, known as *casetas*. They've gotten pretty fancy, with wooden floors, bars, kitchens, portable toilets, café tables, and a dance floor where locals will show off their skill at the complex, two-person dance know as the *sevillanas*. Most tents are private, owned by prominent families, businesses, social clubs, religious associations, and other groups, but there are a few public ones where you can drop in and buy food and *rebujitos* (the classic *Feria* drink of very dry sherry mixed with a soft drink similar to 7up).

Nearly every woman you see will be dressed in a *traje de flamenca* (flamenco outfit) featuring a dress of eye-popping fabric in bold colors and often polka dots, fashioned in what's known as mermaid style: skin tight from bust to knees then erupting in massive ruffles to the ground. In keeping with the livestock tradition, everyone who has access to a horse rides to the fairground or arrives by horse-drawn carriage. At dusk all the horses are required to leave, forming an impromptu parade that's worth the effort to see.

Following a few hours of rest, everyone returns for a late dinner and more dancing. Somewhere toward dawn, they'll stagger homeward, stopping briefly to refuel at a stand selling *churros* (fried dough) and hot chocolate before navigating the stairs to their apartment and falling into bed. Shortly after that, the alarm goes off and they drag themselves off to work. They say that during Feria week, the average Sevillano gets two hours of sleep a night. I'm amazed it's that much.

At Pentecost (another Catholic liturgical holy day, held on the Sunday that falls closest to 49 days after Easter, which in 2022 is June 6) you've got the *Romería del Rocío*, a pilgrimage to honor a sacred effigy of the Virgin in a vast wooded park 50 miles south of the city. Participants wear colorful traditional clothes and sturdy boots to walk the distance or ride in an ox-drawn cart like a covered wagon festooned with flowers. The journey takes three days in each direction, and naturally they party under the stars in fields along the way. I'm told one euphemism for sex, *echar polvo* (to toss up dust) refers to the many courting couples frolicking in the darkness beyond the pilgrimage campfires.

Participating in the *Romería del Rocío* is complicated and costly, but you can easily join in the fun by watching the pilgrims gather for the departure, which is likely to be early on the morning of June 3 (check local newspapers or online to confirm the details). Various groups leave from different neighborhoods of the city and from towns and villages throughout the region. I usually see them off in Triana, a neighborhood across the river where the pilgrims traditionally gather in the little street between Santa Ana (the church) and Santa Ana (the bar). Many will pop into the bar for a shot of *anis seco* (a very dry aniseed liqueur that tastes like paint thinner), a customary morning eye-opener.

On June 16, 2022 the city will celebrate *Corpus Christi* (Body of Christ), carrying the communion bread through the streets in a spectacular gold display called a monstrance. The center point is Plaza San Francisco, where a portal and huge altar will be set up, flanked by statues including San Fernando, the king who recaptured Seville for Christian Spain in 1248 and was declared a saint for his efforts. (Two weeks earlier, on May 30, a special mass at the cathedral honors San Fernando; it's the one day a year you can see his 750-year-old mummified remains displayed behind the altar. The fact they haven't crumbled to dust is viewed as a miracle.) All over the city people put up smaller altars in their neighborhood and stage their own little *Corpus Christi* processions. Branches of rosemary are strewn in front of altars and in the streets where the main procession will pass, so priests and attendants step on the rosemary, releasing the heavenly scent into the balmy air.

In May and June the kids have their moment when they stage the *Cruz de Mayo* (May Cross) processions with little homemade platforms, often cobbled together from a card table, a cross made of sticks, and purple fabric. The neighborhood boys (some of them quite small) carry the platforms while the girls work the crowd, asking for donations to cover the modest costs of the enterprise. Donations are put into cans, which the girls rattle to solicit money, giving rise to the expression *dar la lata* (to give the can) which means to annoy someone. But to tell the truth, it's far from annoying. I find the whole scene pretty adorable, especially when the inevitable lurching and toppling occurs. There's no set schedule, but if you're in town, you're more than likely to see a few *Cruz de Mayo* processions wandering by.

Sizzling summers

In July and August, the weather is so hot that nobody schedules anything.

Relentless stretches of triple digit temperatures force people indoors from lunchtime until dark. When the sun sets, everyone emerges ready to eat, drink, and make merry with outdoor concerts and movies, bars that stay open until dawn, and playgrounds full of children. Friends from the US protest, aghast, at seeing little kids on swings at midnight, but hey, they need to exercise at hours when they won't risk heatstroke.

Heat-related illness is a genuine risk here in summer. Seville is the warmest city in Continental Europe, and now, thanks to climate change, the summers keep getting longer and hotter. In fact, sizzling temperatures have become so severe that Seville recently made headlines around the world by announcing it will start ranking its heat waves and assigning them names, like hurricanes and tropical storms.

Naturally we're all agog to learn what they'll be called. Naming weather patterns goes back to ancient times when everyone was hoping to appease a god or invoke the aid of a saint. In the 19th century, a British meteorologist in Australia, Clement Wragge, kicked off modern storm naming by calling particularly nasty cyclones after government officials he disliked. Will our mayor do the same? Naming starts in 2022; watch my blog for the juicy details.

Fall and the year-end holidays

The summer heat now lasts well into October, with daytime

temperatures in the 80s and nights too warm for comfortable sleep. There are no local fall festivals, although Halloween, which was unheard of here when I first arrived, has captured the imaginations of local families, and you'll find clusters of school children running around dressed as witches, ghouls, and goblins.

The weather cools in early November, with lows in the upper 40s and 50s and highs around 70. To extend the outdoor dining season, which is more popular than ever with Covid-conscious visitors and locals, the owners of many restaurants and bars will surround the tables with heaters.

About this time you'll notice holiday decorations going up all over town. Until ten years ago, all I saw were banners of Baby Jesus and stuffed figures of the Three King, hung from balconies on rope ladders, as if they were sneaking in to leave their gifts. Now Santas and decorated trees have become fashionable in public places and in the homes of trendier residents. In early December the holiday lights are lit; you'll find particularly lavish displays overhead on Avenida de la Constitución by the cathedral and in Plaza San Salvador.

But what Sevillanos really look forward to all year are the Nativity scenes (known as *belenes*, from the word "Bethlehem"). You'll find *belenes* everywhere: churches, shops, government buildings, and (if you're lucky enough to be invited) in the homes of friends, where they may occupy the entire guest bedroom from wall to wall. Sevillanos feel the magnitude of the occasion requires far, far more than just a stable and the Holy Family; many *belenes* include hundreds of figurines, the entire town of Bethlehem, Roman ruins, and (as a backdrop for the flight into Egypt) pyramids and the Sphinx.

If you look closely in the dark corners, you may discover a crouching *caganer*, a figure who is clearly defecating. Yes, you read that right. This earthy realism is meant to remind us that we don't have to be perfect to be part of something miraculous. The tradition has launched a side industry of celebrity *caganers*, from Darth Vader to Madonna (the singer) to political and sports stars.

Belenes can include all sorts of other quirky elements. I've seen a shepherd "urinating" real water, a donkey giving birth, GI Joe figures gathered reverently around a manger (at the Army Navy store), the Holy Family nestled inside an old drum-style washing machine (at the dry cleaners), and one with live baby rabbits, ducks, and songbirds inside a church. For several glorious years one of the large candy manufacturers created the town of Bethlehem out of 1500 kilos of chocolate and a river of honey in which floated white chocolate swans. I know, right? My idea of heaven.

Christmas Day isn't the culmination of the season; that comes on January 6, which I'll describe in a moment. On December 24th families gather for a feast, and on the 25th there's not much scheduled, although commercial establishments, including nearly all restaurants, will be closed.

Families gather again to ring in the New Year together, with two rituals that absolutely must be observed to ensure good luck in the coming year. One is the wearing of *bragas rojas* (red underpants) beneath your street clothes; ideally you're supposed to receive them as a gift. Didn't bring any with you? Don't worry, they're on offer in every clothing, department, and discount store throughout Seville, in every conceivable style from nice to very naughty indeed.

On December 31st of 2019, Rich and I were at the home of Spanish friends, and I was horrified to realize, shortly before midnight, that in my rush to get ready for the evening's festivities, I had forgotten to don my *bragas rojas*. I've carefully observed this tradition for many years, knowing that we all need to safeguard our good luck any way we can.

"How could I have forgotten?" I wailed to Rich on the walk home. "Sure hope this doesn't mean 2020 will be a dud."

Was what followed all my fault? If so, I've certainly learned my lesson! The following New Year's Eve I put on my *bragas rojas* and wrote a blog post urging all my readers to adopt this tradition to ensure our luck doesn't ever get that bad again. I hope you'll join me in this effort.

The other way to ensure good fortune involves consuming twelve grapes, one at each tolling of the clock at midnight. For every one you swallow at the right moment, you'll have a month of good luck in the coming year.

Warning #1: it's impossible to get your grapes down fast enough unless you peel them first. I know you won't believe me until you try this for yourself, but trust me, you'll find yourself choking by the third or fourth grape.

Warning #2: skinning small, round, slippery fruit takes some practice, especially after several glasses of *cava* (Spanish bubbly). Nowadays, I do what so many Spaniards do: I buy special cans that contain twelve peeled, waterlogged grapes that are perfect for chugging.

I naturally assumed that the grape tradition sprang from some saint's miracle or an edict by King Alfonso the Wise in the 13th century, but eventually I learned it was born from modern commercial greed. In 1909 the grape growers of Alicante had such a surplus that in desperation they came up with this new "tradition" as a way to get the public to take the extras off their hands. Those grape growers must have been wearing extra-powerful red underwear that year, because it caught on in a huge way, and ever since then, downing 12 grapes at midnight has defined New Year's Eve in Spain and in many other Spanish-speaking countries.

The last big celebration rolls around on January 6, known in the Catholic liturgical calendar as Epiphany, the day the *Reyes Magos* (Three Kings) brought gifts to the Christ child. Today these generous guys return each year to bring gifts to good kids of all ages, and on the eve of that happy event, there's a huge parade called the *Cabalgata*. The 33 floats have such kid-friendly themes as Cinderella, Harry Potter, and of course, each of the Three Kings: Gaspar, Melchor and Balthasar, played by prominent members of the community who pay handsomely for the privilege. The crews are mostly kids, who have a ball flinging 176,000 pounds of candy to the boisterous crowd. There are many splendid vantage points; I usually watch from opposite the church Santa María Magdalena (Calle San Pablo 12), which provides a gorgeous backdrop for photos.

Do Sevillanos ever work?

As I was writing this chapter, my long-time reader Faye asked, "Do people actually work in Seville? From your blogs it sounds like one big street party there." I could certainly see how she got that impression!

"Yes, people do work here," I reassured her, "and take their jobs seriously. The big difference is that they balance those jobs with their family and social life, and don't always give work top priority. You're expected to spend quantity and quality time with people you care about on a regular basis, rather than fitting them into the margins of your life. The city's vibrant street life is the place visitors and locals can most easily intersect, so that's what I tend to write about."

Sevillanos have a more Mediterranean approach to life, one that often surprises first-time visitors. Having weathered thousands of years of astounding triumphs and crushing disasters, the city has learned to focus on what truly matters: spending time with the people we love, enjoying small pleasures, and doing our bit to add to the joyful noise of the world.

Major Fiestas and Holidays in Seville 2022

January 1, New Year's Day

January 6, Reyes Magos (Three Kings Day)

February 14, Valentine's Day

February 20, Seville Marathon

February 28, Andalucía Day

April 10 – 17, Semana Santa (Holy Week)

April 17, Easter and start of bullfighting season

May 1, Mother's Day

May 1 – 7, Feria de Abril (April Fair)

May 2, Labor Day

June 6, El Rocío pilgrimage

June 16, Corpus Christi

August 15, Assumption of the Virgin

September 22, Feria de San Miguel bullfights

October 12, National Day of Spain

November 1, All Saints' Day

December 6, Spanish Constitution Day

December 8, Immaculate Conception Day

December 25, Christmas Day

December 31, New Year's Eve

3.
HOW CAN I CHECK SPAIN'S ENTRY REQUIREMENTS?

Spain, like most countries, keeps scrambling to devise regulations that can keep their residents safe while welcoming visitors and their much-needed money. Changes in the pandemic, and our understanding of how to deal with it, result in new rules at seemingly random intervals. At the moment I'm writing this, Americans wishing to enter Spain on the usual 90-day tourist visa must be fully vaxxed. This means having the second dose no less than 14 days and no more than nine months prior to arrival in Spain; if your second dose was longer ago than that, you'll need to show proof of a booster more than 14 days prior to travel.

Other travelers — including citizens and legal residents of Spain, the European Union, and the Schengen Area — have less stringent requirements. In the months before Omicron, regulations had become more relaxed, and Americans were allowed into Spain as long as they could prove they'd been vaccinated, had a negative test within the last 72 hours, or had survived Covid. And that may soon be the case again, if Covid doesn't spring any more surprises on us.

You'll need to know the current regulations and prepare the required documents in advance of your trip. As Spain is particularly prone to announcing changes at the last minute, you'll want to check out current regulations now, double check later, then check again as your departure date approaches.

Where to check online

The official word on entry requirements is supposed to come out of Spain's Ministry of Health, but even with the English translation, the site is so convoluted it's difficult to make much sense of it. You'll find clearer information on the site of the US Embassy and Consulate in Spain and Andorra. Go to their Covid page, but — and this is a very, very important heads-up — the first section is all about entering the US from Spain, which has completely different requirements. Scroll down a little to the section marked Country-Specific Information and you'll find the latest details on getting into Spain from the US.

You may need to do similar research on other countries' entry requirements as well, if your route to Seville requires a stopover. There are few flights between the US and Seville, and even fewer direct ones, so you may find your best route takes you through another nation. Naturally this means complying with all their regulations, which may or may not be similar to Spain's. A good place to find out more is JoinSherpa, which lists current entry requirements for countries around the world.

Everyone entering Spain is now required to fill out a health control document, known as the FCS form, which can be found on the Spanish government's website at spth.gob.es. The FCS form can only be completed 48 hours in advance of departure, as it requires information such as your flight and seat numbers, which are subject to last-minute changes. Once you've submitted this form, you'll receive the Documental Control QR code you need to get into the country.

Once you have verified the requirements, you'll want to prepare the paperwork ahead of time. And I do mean literal paperwork; be sure to print out all documents, even if it's just a QR code. Younger travelers, steeped in the conventions of the digital age, may scoff at this, but you don't want to risk missing your flight because you forgot to charge your phone, accidentally erased something, had your phone stolen, or ran into some other unexpected glitch.

No matter how carefully you prepare, you can expect to be

surprised at some point along the way. A friend who just flew from New York to Madrid was pulled out of line upon arrival and told he was one of 30 randomly selected passengers who had to take a rapid Covid test before being allowed into Spain. Luckily it came out negative. Whew!

When Rich and I traveled from San Francisco to Seville in September of 2021, the regulations and requirements were slightly different, but the process was essentially the same, so our story will give you some idea what to expect.

Our journey from SF to Seville

The best route we could find required a London stopover, which added many hours, gallons of coffee, and handfuls of aspirin to the research and preparations. We had to land in Heathrow, and while we remained inside our section of the airport we would have in-transit status, requiring specific forms attesting to our health status (described below). But if we left the designated section of the airport, we would officially enter the UK and become liable for all sorts of other Covid restrictions, possibly including quarantine. Yikes! Obviously we didn't want to do that.

Unfortunately, there are no flights between Heathrow and Seville. In the past, we've often taken the shuttle bus to Gatwick, which does have service to Seville, but that was now out of the question.

Luckily we could fly from Heathrow into Málaga, which is only 125 miles from Seville, with a good railway connection.

For in-transit passengers, the UK required a Covid test within 72 hours of the flight. But not just any old Covid test. According to the official website, "The test must meet performance standards of ≥97% specificity, ≥80% sensitivity at viral loads above 100,000 copies/ml. This could include tests such as a nucleic acid test, including a PCR test, a LAMP test, or an antigen test, such as an LFD (lateral flow device) test." Pretending we knew what any of that meant, Rich and I contacted various clinics in an effort to secure the right tests at the right time and, if possible, for the right price. Fees went as high as $300 per person, but luckily our friend John tipped us off to a free pop-up test center at a CVS in San Francisco, which sent results sent to our phones within half an hour. Thanks for that, John!

A comment on my blog gave us a heads-up about the UK's other monster requirement. My friend Jackie, author of the lively blog TravelnWrite, wrote, "Good luck! We just returned to the States via London. In addition to that test, make sure you have filled out your PLF, passenger locator form. It is required even for the shortest of layovers — ours was two hours long and it took nearly that long to fill out the four-page form."

I thought she was exaggerating — you know how we bloggers love a bit of drama — but if anything Jackie was understating the case. Working online in the comfort of our dining room (aka transportation planning hub), Rich and I spent ages filling in our passport numbers, Covid history, travel details including seat numbers on every flight, phone numbers, and more. What, no eye exam or letter from the priest? Because it required up-to-the-minute travel information such as seat assignments, the PLF couldn't be completed until 48 hours before our flight, adding a zippy note of suspense to the proceedings.

For Spain, we needed a Documental Control QR code attesting to our vaccination status. This online form could only be completed 48 hours before our flight, at which time they would let us know about any additional entry requirements. I spent weeks fretting about what they might want — an essay in Spanish about why I wanted to go to Seville? An oath of loyalty? A whopping extra service fee? But in the end, they mostly wanted to know if we were vaxxed. *¡Sí, totalmente!*

All the hours we put into the legwork and paperwork paid off. We breezed through check-in at SFO, producing document after document, including printouts of our test results, the UK's PLF, and Spanish QR codes, and in return we received boarding passes for both flights. We were on our way!

The late afternoon flight out of SFO was about half full, and we expected to sleep much of the next ten and a half hours. Then a woman sat down nearby with an infant who had a set of lungs like Pavarotti and the staying power of an Olympic athlete. Hearing about it afterward, my friend Bob wrote, "Sorry you had to listen to the screaming baby. It conjures the old aphorism: 'The plane to Spain can make one go insane!'" Amen to that, Bob.

Except for the baby, everyone was scrupulous about face masks — so scrupulous, in fact, that during the safety demonstration, the flight attendant had to tell people, "Remove your face mask before you put on the oxygen mask." I think we can all agree that's good advice!

Arriving in Heathrow, which is filled with insistent, obnoxious marketing and restless crowds, Rich and I decided to splurge on a pay-to-use lounge called Club Aspire, which is open to anyone. Or at least, anyone who is willing to cough up $33 for the luxury of sitting on comfortable furniture in a quiet room, enjoying free coffee and scones with clotted cream while plugging in a laptop and maybe dozing off now and then.

Five hours later, we boarded the plane to Málaga. To make us feel at home, they'd seated us near another screaming baby, but by then, who cared?

A few noisy hours later we stumbled off the flight, zipped through customs, checked into our hotel. Minutes later we'd found a small backstreet tapas bar. As we sipped ice-cold Cruzcampo beer and nibbled thin slivers of *jamón Iberico* (the best Spanish ham), we kept exclaiming, "We're back! We're really here! We're in Spain!" The next day we slept late, hopped a train to Seville, and made it home at last.

Transportation alternatives

That was the route that worked best for us, but you may want to consider other options. Some of our friends like to fly into Lisbon, take the train south to Faro, and take the bus to Seville. You can cover that entire route in seven or eight hours, but an evening's layover in Lisbon and another Faro will make for a more interesting and relaxing journey. Others fly into Madrid and continue to Seville by high-speed train, a pleasant two and a half hours in which to snooze away some jet lag.

And then there's the option of driving the last leg of your journey. Between Spain's well-maintained highways and your GPS, you won't have any trouble getting to Seville. But once you're there, be advised that driving becomes a nightmare of biblical proportions. The downtown area is a rabbit warren of narrow, winding streets designed in medieval times to confuse and delay invading armies. To make matters worse, a recent mayor's efforts to make the city more friendly to pedestrians and bicycles caused many major thoroughfares to become off-limits to cars, putting tremendous strain on smaller roads. You're likely to snake dizzyingly through town without ever getting near your hotel, eventually realizing with horror that you are back onto the ring road for the third or fourth time. My advice: park on the outskirts (for instance at the Plaza de Armas or the Santa Justa Railway Station) and proceed on foot or by taxi.

However you arrive in Seville, I suggest that the first thing you do is find a place to recombobulate over a cup of coffee (or other beverage). Rich and I do this whenever we arrive in a new town. The ritual is, of course, less about coffee than about catching our breath, making sure we know where we're going, and if necessary locating a cash machine so we can get enough local currency for our immediate needs, like taxi fare to the hotel. Collecting our wits this way leaves us better prepared for the adventure ahead.

4.
WHAT'S THE BEST WAY TO EXPLORE THE CITY?

Seville is great for walking, almost perfectly flat with wonderful old architecture and charming vistas to keep you entertained as you get lost. And you will get lost. Even using the GPS on your phone, sooner or later (most likely sooner) you'll find yourself on a street corner saying in exasperation, "But it should be right here!" And most likely the hotel, museum, or ancient monument you're seeking is quite nearby but is cleverly concealing itself on a parallel street that is so narrow it defeats the ability of the world's most sophisticated technology to detect it. Luckily there are sidewalk cafés just about everywhere, so you can always recombobulate over a cup of coffee and try again.

If you ask for directions, you'll find the locals are quite helpful; most likely they will direct you to a nearby plaza and then tell you to ask again. They are not being lazy or withholding information, they are simply being realistic about how complicated it will be just to get you to that plaza. If by some miracle you make it that far, they know your best bet is to have someone else point you in the right direction from there.

Some days I love nothing better than wandering about aimlessly and getting lost in a strange city. But it can also be intensely frustrating, and Rich and I often turn to an app called Triposo for a guided route through a strange town. For navigating Seville, there are many apps to choose from, including GPSMyCity, Triposo, and the city's own Seville APP. These will help you follow a route that will take you to some of the city's finest landmarks and give you a little background on each. It's a good way to start finding your way around.

For more a more nuanced introduction to the city, you may want to consider finding a local guide. All sorts of private individuals and major tour groups are available in the city now; you can find full details, prices, and reviews online. Since most of these services only became available long after I moved here and knew my way around, I haven't tried them. But I can tell you about two people I know who can be counted on to show you interesting sides of the city few tourists ever see.

Food tours

Seven years ago, an expat pal asked me, "Would you and Rich

be interested in going on the test run for a new food tour a friend of mine is starting here in Seville?"

Tough work, but somebody has to do it!

"If it'll help," I replied graciously.

Rich and I met up with Lauren Aloise and a small group of fellow volunteers to spend three hours strolling through the city's back streets, nibbling and sipping, in what would become Tastes, Tapas & Traditions of Seville, the flagship food tour of Lauren's company Devour Seville.

We sampled slivers of freshly cut *jamón* (ham), orange-flavored almond cookies baked by nuns, fried sand shark marinated in cumin and vinegar, and other treats. Mostly we grazed on the hoof, but from time to time we settled around a table for heartier fare, such as the robust *mantecado de lomo al whiskey*. I've often enjoyed *lomo al whiskey*, which is pork loin in a garlicky whiskey sauce, usually accompanied by French fries and a small basket of bread for sopping up any leftover sauce. Here, they combined it all in one huge sandwich. I have to admit I was skeptical. French fries inside a sandwich? Why, that's flying in the face of nature! But I had to admit it tasted amazing.

Best of all, the tour included plenty of stories. Seville is abundantly blessed with outrageous myths, legends, and ancient superstitions, and as Lauren led us through the city's markets, convent sweet shops, and back street cafés, she regaled us with her favorites. (More about these stories a little later in this book.) It was a wonderful sampling of the city's cultural history. The food tour's route has changed over the years — I just read the current itinerary, and my mouth is watering all over again — and Devour Seville now has several tour leaders and itineraries exploring different aspects of the city's culinary life.

Later, when I interviewed Lauren for my blog, she told me, "I started freelance writing about food and travel, and gave cooking classes. One day I found an ad for a food tour in France and thought it sounded perfect. Food tours combine amazing food, local history and culture, and support for small businesses — what's not to love? I could step away from the computer and actually show people the types of things I was already writing about. So I just dove in." And I'm so glad she did!

Boutique guide service

If you're looking for a more comprehensive introduction to the city, you might consider working with my friend Sarah Gemba, an American who discovered Seville during a semester abroad. "I was an innocent 19-year-old college student who was thrown into a beautiful, exotic city," she told me when I interviewed her for my blog. "I loved every minute of it.

The only thing that annoyed me was that I was a *guiri* (the Spanish term of endearment for a foreigner) and I wanted to be one of the fun-loving Sevillanos." She made the transition soon after college, returning to Seville to work in the cultural travel sector before founding her boutique travel service, Spain Savvy.

Friends of mine who have toured the city with Sarah can't say enough good things about her. She great with logistics, knows all the best places to eat, and helps people get in on the fun of the festivals — for instance, showing them how to dress up for the *Feria* and arranging for them to arrive by horse-drawn carriage. "My clients are anywhere from two to eighty years old; some of my favorite clients are families with small children," said Sarah, who has three kids of her own with her Spanish husband, Daniel. "My clients are interested in luxury or adventure travel. They are curious travelers who like to eat well and discover the hidden corners of their destinations. They speak a little Spanish but are yearning to learn more. They want to meet locals and learn what it would be like to live (or retire) here."

When I asked her what advice she'd give first-time visitors, Sarah said, "Erase any pre-conceived notions you might have about Spain and prepare to be dazzled. This country will truly surprise you in so many ways. Do a bit of research and reading, and brush up on your iool Spanish so you can connect with the locals. If you are friendly, they will respond with a tremendous amount of warmth and welcome!"

Finding your own way

Not everyone wants a guide, and if you prefer to go it on your own, Seville makes it easy to cover the essentials. There are only two absolutely must-see landmarks, the kind you'd be embarrassed to admit you never got around to: the cathedral and the Alcázar palace. They're conveniently located across from each other in the heart of the city, but it's better not to try and jam both of them into a single day as touring them properly can take hours. With 2022 shaping up to be a boom year for tourism, be sure to order tickets online in advance.

At the Alcázar, you'll want to linger in the palace with its gorgeous Moorish-style architecture, then stroll through the splendid grounds, which appeared in *Game of Thrones* as the water gardens of Dorne. For the cathedral, sign up for the rooftop tour (unless you have mobility issues or vertigo; there are a lot of steps and dizzying heights) for a very different, behind-the-scenes perspective. If wandering around the cathedral on your own, be sure to visit the Treasury and, if you're able, climb the series of ramps that go up inside the Giralda tower, which offers a bird's eye view of the city.

After covering those two spectacular landmarks, you can relax and explore other sights at your leisure. You might enjoy the Museo de Bellas Artes (Fine Arts Museum), the Palacio de Las Dueñas (home of the late Duquesa de Alba, Spain's richest and most titled aristocrat), Parque Maria Luisa, and the Plaza de España. The city's newest landmark is the Metropol Parasol, which everyone calls Las Setas (The Mushrooms), a hideous, overblown, sixties-style structure that went up a few years ago, at enormous expense, in Plaza de la Encarnacíon. Inside, on the ground floor, is one of the city's major food markets; older food markets can be visited on Calle Feria and just across the river in Triana at the end of the Isabel II bridge.

Exploring the shops

If shopping is on your to-do list, head to the main retail district centered around three parallel streets: Sierpes, Tetuán and Cuna. They're lined with international chain stores, such as Zara, Mango, and H&M, but you'll still find plenty of old-style shops too, selling hats, stationary, jewelry, and sweets; if you wander off onto the side streets, you'll discover high-end boutiques and quirkier stores of all kinds. Don't miss the city's giant department store, El Corte Inglés, which has branches in Plaza Duque and Plaza Magdalena, and offers everything from smart clothes to housewares to hardware to a gourmet supermarket. They have a huge new sporting goods section, but it doesn't begin to rival the vast Decathlon store nearby on Calle Martín Villa.

Just outside the prime shopping zone, you'll find discount stores selling everything from groceries to clothing to housewares to toys to … you get the idea. These bazaars, which began appearing about ten years ago, are run by the Chinese community, causing locals to dub them, with more clarity than ethnic sensitivity, "chinos." The term has become so embedded in the language that now many stores incorporate the word in their name. These bazaars are fun to browse through and a godsend for tourists, locals, and expats in search of bargains, or anyone who needs to buy something during the midday break, as most remain open all day.

While larger downtown stores and some supermarkets stay open continuously, typically from 10:00 am to 9:00 pm, smaller and more traditional shops, along with all government offices, banks, and many other businesses, close from 2:00 to 5:00 pm for lunch and siesta. During the crushing heat of July and August, many shops don't reopen at all in the afternoon, and some close down entirely for several weeks to allow everyone to take a vacation. In such cases you'll often find a hand-lettered notice about "*discanso del personal*" (staff resting).

Throughout every shopping district, you'll find a scattering of cafés, bakeries, and small restaurants, so when you've shopped your fill, you can, as the Spanish put it, *reanimarse* (reanimate yourself) with a sip and a nibble. Here in Seville, every meal — even the most casual snack — is regarded the most important of the day.

5.
WHY DO SEVILLANOS EAT
FIVE MEALS A DAY?

When I first read that Spanish nutritionists recommend eating five meals a day as a weight-loss strategy, I knew I was on to something. I immediately got up from my desk, went to the kitchen, and made myself a snack to munch on while digesting this wisdom.

The author of one article insisted that early breakfast, mid-morning second breakfast, lunch, afternoon *merienda* (snack), and dinner are all essential for anyone hoping to avoid overeating at any one meal. Not only that, she warned, "To lose this traditional schedule is to throw open the doors to indiscriminate nibbling." Gadzooks! Not that!

Our best bet, she said, is to spend more time at the table, eating slowly in a relaxed manner, so our brains and bodies have time to appreciate the meal and absorb the fact that we've consumed enough nutrition to make it through the next few hours until it's time to eat again. The author reported, in a tone verging on horror, that Americans typically allot just 50 minutes a day to the pleasures of the table — which may not actually involve a table at all, but can take place in a car, at a work station, or (and clearly it pained the author even to mention this) while walking. In the UK, the average time consuming sustenance is an even more paltry 39 minutes. *Gracias a Dios*, the Spanish continue to spend a civilized one hour and forty-five minutes a day at meals, while the French manage two solid hours *à la table.*

Why the French and Spanish don't get fat

As we all learned from Mireille Guiliano's bestseller *French Women Don't Get Fat, les Français* are not spending those hours nibbling lettuce leaves and rice cakes. They're tucking into all the good stuff we're told to deny ourselves when trying to slim down: chocolate, cheese, meat, bread, even (gasp!) butter. So why don't they get fat? In large part because *les Français* pace themselves. They take pleasure in consuming modest amounts of delicious food five times a day, rising from the table satisfied in body and soul, yet already entertaining agreeable thoughts about the next delicious installment.

"French women," says Guiliano, "think about good things to eat; American women typically worry about bad things to eat."

When I asked my French friend Sandra about this one morning over cups of *café con leche*, she said, "It's true. We look forward to eating with the same pleasure that we look forward to meeting a good friend."

In America, we tend to view breakfast, lunch, and dinner as legitimate nutritional intake, while consigning morning and afternoon snacks to the category of "cheating," a sign of physical weakness if not outright moral failure. When I first came to Spain, I was astonished to see, between 10:00 and 11:00 in the morning, seemingly everyone in the city heading to cafés for a midmorning second breakfast of coffee and small toasted baguettes dripping with olive oil and topped with slivers of ham.

This modest repast tides them over until lunch at 2:00, which for many is the main meal of the day and may include a small beer or *tinto de verano* (an iced drink of red wine mixed with a soft drink similar to 7up), which is a great way to ease into the afternoon siesta. Around 5:00 everyone pours back into the cafés to refresh themselves via *merienda*, typically sweet rolls and yet more coffee, before heading back to the office for three more hours of work. Dinner comes at around 9:00 or later.

I was stunned when I first learned about this schedule. Five meals a day? Had they no shame? And why, I wondered, weren't my new *amigos* obese, jittery wrecks? In fact, they all appeared to be reasonably sane and healthy — and would, according to the statistical tables, live nearly four years longer than the average American.

Like the French, *los Españoles* tend to eat frequently and moderately, comfortable in the knowledge that another meal is always just around the corner. With food and rest occurring at reliable intervals, they never seem to worry about storing up fuel for the long haul or missing a little sleep in a good cause, such as dinner.

In southern Spain, dinners start late and often last until the small hours of the morning. When visiting someone's home for the evening meal, I settle in knowing I'll be at the table until well past midnight. Only then will my hostess signal the beginning of the end by producing the dessert, usually an enormous, frothy, gooey confection piled high with whipped cream. At such moments I am always staggered by the fact that nobody ever recoils, exclaiming, "Oh no, I couldn't possibly!" Instead, every man and woman at the table leans forward exclaiming, with what appears to be genuine pleasure, *"Que rico!"* (How rich!) Having been raised by parents and grandparents who remembered The Hunger, those long, lean years after the Spanish Civil War when nobody had nearly enough to eat, my Seville friends still tend to view every delicious calorie as cause for celebration.

Living in Spain, I've become more and more intrigued by what food tell us about what's been going on and how everyone feels about it. For instance, the ever-popular *cola de toro* (bull's tail stewed in wine) is part of Andalucía's Roman heritage and ancient bullfighting traditions, both sources of deep local pride. Rabbits are always displayed in the market intact and with their fur on, a custom dating back to The Hunger, when a housewife wanted to be sure the butcher wasn't selling her the neighbor's cat (or her own). With history like that, it's no wonder Sevillanos take the occasional shortages and supply chain hiccoughs in stride.

Where shall we go to eat?

Giving each meal the respect it deserves, Sevillanos are apt to deliberate carefully over where to go for the best food at the best price — and then, more than likely, they'll wind up at their customary neighborhood tapas bar. Here they'll feel comfortable knowing they're in the warm embrace of those who support the same *futbol* team (Sevilla or their blue-collar archrival Betis), march in the same *Semana Santa* procession, and agree that newfangled avocado toast doesn't belong on the breakfast table.

One thing all Seville eateries have in common: they've adapted to pandemic conditions. Wait staff and cooks all wear masks; customers usually don't unless they're heading to the back in search of *los servicios* (restrooms). Inside tables are spaced further apart, and outdoor seating is in such high demand that tables have spread to every available square meter of sidewalk. There are even a few parklets around, although sacrificing parking spaces to outdoor dining is hotly contested in crowded neighborhoods. Most places disinfect (or at least wipe down) the tables between customers. You'll find QR codes for the menus posted prominently, usually pasted on a corner of the table, although if you ask, your *camarero* (waiter) or *camarera* (waitress) may bring out a printed version or point you to a chalkboard on the wall. Lots have hand sanitizer around in case you didn't bring your own.

When Omicron hit hard in December of 2021, new regulations required everyone entering a restaurant, bar, or café to show proof of vaccination in the form of a QR code — commonly called a Covid passport — issued by the public health system and kept handy on mobile phones. Don't have an EU Covid passport? Not to worry, your vaccine card from the US or most other countries will suffice. I copied mine and had the copy laminated, so I can leave the original in a safe place and still present documents on request; I do the same with my residency card, which lets me get in free to local monuments.

This came in handy in January, when the Alcázar palace was nearly deserted in the post-holiday lull. Rich and I decided to stop in for a coffee, as we used to do before it got so crowded that visiting meant advance reservations and tedious long lines. We made a beeline for the garden café, one of the loveliest spots in the city to linger over a *café con leche*. When we walked inside the café to order, the barista asked for our Covid passports. Rich misheard him and pulled out his Alcazar entrance ticket. The barista glanced at the ticket's QR code from four feet away, accepted it without scanning or questions, and waved me through as well, even though I hadn't shown him anything.

Unfortunately, this is not an isolated incident; QR codes are not always examined scrupulously. Occasionally they may even be bogus; police just broke up a fake Covid passport ring involving 1600 people in Madrid and Barcelona. It would be comforting to believe that every single person in every Spanish restaurant is well and fully vaxxed, but sadly there are no guarantees. Luckily nearly all the eateries mentioned in this guide offer outdoor seating; I've noted the few that don't. Heaters are hauled out during the mild winter and early spring, so people can linger comfortably over early morning coffee or late dinners.

Breakfast (first and second)

Your culinary day starts, of course, with *desayuno* (breakfast).

The phrase "breakfast is the most important meal of the day" was coined by 19th century cereal manufacturers, most probably John Harvey Kellogg, a religious zealot who believed eating breakfast cereal would make Americans strong enough to stop thinking about sex. (It didn't. Go figure.) The Spanish, who have no such Puritan goals, enjoy their version of breakfast so much they indulge in it twice every morning, with great enthusiasm.

At home, Sevillanos typically start the day with a first *desayuno* of coffee and toast topped with olive oil and ham or butter and jam. They then head to their workplace and put in an hour or two of labor, after which they'll refresh themselves with a midmorning break at a nearby café, enjoying another round of coffee and toast to fortify themselves until lunch.

To accommodate the second-breakfast habit, the city has café-bars on practically every block. Some are grand, an increasing number are corporate efforts, and the hipsters outdo one another in providing quirky environments, flat whites, and wifi workspaces. But the mainstay continues to be modest little neighborhood places you wouldn't look at twice in the US. To American eyes, plain white tables and plastic chairs suggest mass-produced, substandard food, and a back alley location would be another red flag, but those rules of thumb do not hold true in

Seville. The locals love small, inexpensive neighborhood places that have been around for years, with traditional cooking and tiny tables for intimate conversations. Here are some I love for first and/or second breakfast.

Bar Alfalfa, *C. Candilejo 1*, a cozy neighborhood hangout just off Plaza de la Alfalfa; indoor only

El Algabeño, *Calle Arrayan 2*, tucked behind the Feria market so you can shop afterwards

Cafeteria Catunambu, *Calle Sierpes 10* , offering good coffee and great people-watching

Bar Commercial, *C. Lineros 9*, famous for its *churros* (fried dough) and chocolate

Un Gato en Bicicleta, *Calle Pérez Galdós 2*, a hipster charmer filled with books and art; indoor only

Café Hércules, *Calle Peris Mencheta 15*, a bohemian café serving avocado toast

Otto Café, *Plaza Monte Sion 8*, a chic little spot just off Calle Feria

El Pilar, *Avenida José Laguillo 4*, the one Rich and I go to for *churros*

XIX, *Calle Tomás de Ibarra 9*, super fancy yet hip; good for romantic morning-afters; indoor only

So what's everybody ordering for their second breakfast? The choices may be simple, but to get it right requires a fair amount of vocabulary. In Seville, you always order your drink first. The classic is *café con leche*, half espresso and half steamed milk. Too much milk for you? Try a *cortado*, a shot of espresso with half as much milk. Need even more of an eye-opener? Ask for a *café solo*, a straight shot of espresso. Prefer something lower octane? *Café Americano* is plain black coffee, and *leche manchada* (literally "stained milk") is half an inch of espresso and plenty of milk.

I've never seen low-fat milk in a Seville restaurant, but hipster and tourist coffee houses may offer milk alternatives. However, be advised that no one will understand a request for *leche de soya* (soy milk), *leche de avena* (oat milk), or the like because everyone knows milk is produced by lactating mammals, not plants; the barrista will be dumfounded by your ignorance although too polite to say so. Ask for *bebida de soya* (soy drink) or *bebida de avena* (oat drink) instead.

You can also order fresh orange juice (*zumo de naranja*), which is sometimes served with a packet of sugar in case you like it extra sweet. Other juices may be available, but they'll almost certainly come out of a bottle.

Breakfast drinks get even more complicated if, like me, you happen to like tea with milk, which is unheard of here. Ask for *té con leche* (tea with milk) and you'll be served a glass of steamed milk with a tea bag in it. If you ask for *té con leche aparte* (tea with milk apart or on the side) they'll bring you tea but not the milk, assuming you'll drink that later in the meal or want it left in the kitchen for some bizarre reason known only to mad foreigners. *Té con leche aparte para añadir* (tea with milk apart to add in) should do the trick, although you may have to repeat it several times to be understood. You can see why I gave up and switched to *café con leche*.

As for food, toast is such a given you don't even have to say *tostada*; you simply order a *media* (half a small baguette) or *entera* (entire small baguette) and name your toppings. The most common are *aceite y jamón* (olive oil and thin slivers of Spanish ham), *tomate* (tomato), which may come sliced or mashed and can be ordered with or without the ham, and *mantequilla y mermelada* (butter and jam). Traditional places will provide a bottle of olive oil so you can drench your toast with it if you feel you need more. Want heartier or more familiar fare, such as eggs, avocado toast, or corn flakes? You may find them in places that cater to out-of-town visitors, especially those clustered around the cathedral and larger hotels, but you won't see a lot of Sevillanos straying from the traditional menu. I once made pancakes for a Spanish house party, and they all looked aghast, took one courtesy bite, and went back to their *tostadas* with sighs of relief.

Some years ago, when I did a post about Spanish breakfasts, my long-time reader Vera wrote in to ask why I didn't mention *churros* and chocolate, and I had to agree this was a serious oversight on my part. My brother Mike, a devout chocaholic, calls this "Seville's breakfast of champions." You order sizzling hot *churros* and dunk them in hot chocolate as dark and dense as pudding. Yes, I agree, this is possibly the most decadent breakfast ever invented and naturally a huge favorite with the Sevillanos. It's mostly a Sunday indulgence but they'll occasionally have some to *reanimarse* (reanimate themselves) en route home from a party at six in the morning or for afternoon *marienda*, which is essentially a third breakfast. I can only imagine how John Harvey Kellogg is turning in his grave at the very idea of all that pleasure packed into a single meal.

Main meals: lunch and dinner

Where breakfast in Seville has remained fairly old school, lunch and dinner have seen radical changes in recent years as a trendy new foodie culture has swept the city.

When I first arrived in Seville, your choices for lunch and dinner rarely varied; there were a dozen popular dishes such as *carrillada* (stewed pork cheeks), *tortilla de España* (Spanish omelet), and *solomillo al whisky* (pork fillet with whisky sauce). *Paella* and similar rice dishes were only served for Sunday lunch because they take time to prepare properly, should be eaten the moment they're ready, and require a siesta afterwards. (These days, you often see a restaurant advertising five kinds of paella served all day; it's premade, frozen, substandard fare.) Traditional places tend to have interiors with dark wood, old tiles, ham legs hanging from the ceiling, and somebody's *abuela* (grandmother) in the kitchen, making food the way her *abuela* taught her back in the days of Franco and food shortages.

Traditional Sevillano cooking is simple, practical, and thrifty, without innovative flourishes or much in the way of spices. Although families eat vegetables at home, for the most part dining out is a celebration that requires sinking your teeth into meat. Which brings us to Spain's sizzling food controversy.

Last July, Consumer Affairs Minister Alberto Garzón observed, quite rightly, "Eating too much meat is bad for our health and for the planet." As you can imagine, the meat industry exploded with outrage. Spain is the world's fifth largest meat exporter, its citizens are the EU's biggest meat eaters, and *jamón* (ham) is revered as the national dish. This was blasphemy!

Then in late December, as things were finally simmering down, Garzón decided to throw a little gasoline on the fire. After defending traditional grazing methods, he added, "What isn't at all sustainable is these so-called mega-farms. They find a village in a depopulated bit of Spain and put in 4,000, or 5,000 or 10,000 head of cattle. They pollute the soil, they pollute the water, and then they export this poor-quality meat from these ill-treated animals."

In the ensuing uproar, former-lawyer-turned-shepherd María del Camino Limia posted a Facebook video calling Garzón "an ignoramus" and "a puppet at the service of eco-terrorist movements." Naturally her video has gone viral, inflaming the controversy still further. The fuss has been a tremendous boon to newscasters, who are thrilled to report on anything other than Covid statistics, but beyond that, there doesn't seem to be much social impact. Sevillanos are still enthusiastically gathering around great platters of *flamenquín* (slices of *jamón* wrapped in pieces of pork loin, coated in breadcrumb batter, and deep-fried), *pringá* (slow-cooked chorizo, roast pork, and pork fat, served on fluffy rolls), and *jabalí* (wild boar roasted in onions and red wine).

Even the most devoted carnivore may find an entire platter of such hearty fare a bit overwhelming, so you'll be glad to know many traditional dishes can be ordered in various sizes: *tapa* (li appetizer), *media ración* (half portion, about twice the size o *ración* (full portion, a platter suitable for sharing). In pre-pandemic times, sharing food was the norm, and friends would often split even a *tapa* so everyone could try it. Now it's more common to order individual servings to avoid passing germs around, although after the second glass of wine, these concerns often fall by the wayside. One of the beauties of the *tapa* system is that you can start with a small amount, order more if you're still hungry, and stop when your satisfied. A truly civilized way to eat.

When I arrived in Seville more than two decades ago, the old-school recipes were pretty much the only ones on offer. The same dozen dishes were chalked on every menu board, and I knew I could count on a good meal at affordable prices just about anywhere. There are still lots of places like this all over the city, and they are truly wonderful experiences. Some still don't take reservations; in that case, check opening times online and try to get there early. All those shown below have outdoor seating and will do their best to accommodate gluten-free (*sin gluten*) diets or other special requests.

Bar Blanco Cerrillo, *Calle José de Velilla 1*, best *adobo* (marinated fried fish)

Bodeguita Romero, *Calle Harinas 10*, best *carrilladas* (stewed pig cheeks)

Los Coloniales, *Plaza Cristos de Burgos 19*, best *solomillo al whisky* (pork tenderloin)

Casa Morales, *Calle García de Vinuesa 11*, check out the "secret" back bar (entered from the side street)

Returning to Seville in September of 2021, after being gone for 16 months that altered the entire world, I braced myself for a host of unwelcome changes. Being selflessly devoted to keeping my readers informed, I began at once to check out as many taverns, cafés, and restaurants as possible. I was curious (anxious, even) to see who'd weathered the pandemic and who had not. To my surprise, the survival rate was quite high; there were no more casualties than I'd have expected to find after any long absence. But there have been some profound changes to the city's food scene.

At first, I found the city's eateries all insanely crowded. It was a perfect storm. With the last of the pandemic restrictions and curfews removed, pent-up desire drove seemingly everyone out for meals. A long-delayed wedding season finally launched, bringing visitors and endless rounds of festivities in restaurants. The crushing heat of summer was finally easing, so lunch out was a treat again. The net effect: demand was at an all-time high, and even though the city eased regulations to allow for more and more outdoor tables, it was just about impossible to get seated anywhere. I discovered to my dismay that even the smallest and funkiest cafés required advance reservations for lunch and dinner.

After the frantic days of late September, the city settled down a bit, and on weekdays it became possible to drop in for lunch or dinner at many cafés and restaurants. Things got busy again during the holiday season, after which the throngs disappeared due to the usual seasonal drop plus people cancelling trips here due to worries about Omicron. Everyone's expecting an even bigger influx of visitors for the spring festivals, and the city's eateries are gearing up for a boom year.

Adios tapeo,

Sadly, this signals the end to one of Seville's most ancient and beloved traditions, the *tapeo*. Rather like a pub crawl, a *tapeo* involves visiting several bars during the evening, in each of which you order a *tapa* and a drink, usually a *cervecita* (small beer) also called a *caña* (draft beer), which is usually eight ounces and costs about 1.20€ ($1.37). This way you get to sample all sorts of food and various congenial environments while keeping your alcohol consumption fairly modest and getting fresh air and exercise along the way.

In the past, I found my visitors loved the idea of tapas but were easily confused by the concept of a *tapeo*. Although I always explained the idea in elaborate detail before we started, and everyone responded enthusiastically, the plan usually bogged down almost immediately.

"Move on?" they'd say, bewildered, when it was time to leave the first bar. "But we just got here. We've hardly eaten anything. And I've only had a half pint of beer. We can't go yet!" I would point out the next bar was three blocks away and had a specialty they would love, but my words fell on deaf ears. They'd dig in their heels and refuse to budge until the evening was well advanced and the only thing left on the agenda was a nightcap.

For locals and expats living in Seville, the *tapeo* was one of the many cherished pleasures of the city. When Rich and I had dinner with Spanish friends shortly after our return in 2021, I asked, aghast, if every tavern in town now required reservations. "Yes," Julio said sadly. "Spontaneity is gone."

Finding classic Sevillano eateries

Although there are still some great, old-school places in the downtown area, you'll have a better chance of experiencing *Sevilla profunda* (deep Seville) if you go a little further out. I always advise people to stand with their back to the cathedral and walk in any direction for fifteen to twenty minutes and look around. If you're wondering whether you've discovered an authentic, old-school eatery, ask yourself these questions.

Is the place full of Sevillanos? People in the neighborhood know where to find the best food at the best prices. If they're standing three deep at the bar and every outdoor table is jammed with multigenerational family groups, chances are it's worth trying to squeeze in. Sometimes an extra table will be produced on request, so don't be afraid to ask.

Does it belong to a chain? There is a sort of alchemy to corporate ownership that transforms even the freshest ingredients into a sort of gooey sawdust; just think about the last meal you had on a plane or in the hospital. There are decent franchises; I quite like the cheap shrimp and buckets of beer at the La Sureña, a regional chain with locations near the Setas and elsewhere throughout the city. But in general, individually owned places are best.

Are the menus in English? During the pandemic, everyone started using QR codes, so you often have the option to read the menu in Spanish or English; it's fun to watch for translation errors like "pig spit" for pork roasted on a spit. If you find a place with a purely Spanish menu, it may be more of a struggle to order, but you'll know you're off the beaten tourist track.

What's the décor like? Family-owned eateries favor photos of one of the two big *futbol* (soccer) teams, identifiable by red or green jerseys, along with pictures of famous bullfighters, flamenco dancers, *Semana Santa* processions, the *Rocío* pilgrimage, and other local events and celebrities. Look for a small statue of a teenage boy in a colorful toga; that's San Pancracio, the patron saint of health and work, a traditional good-luck gift for those opening a tavern.

How noisy is it? The Spanish love to talk, and when they're enjoying themselves, the buzz of convivial conversation tends to rise. Social distancing of tables mutes this a bit, but there are still lots of places where noise levels require shouting over the din, suggesting that people are having a very good time indeed. You might want to find out what the buzz is all about.

When Rich and I first arrived in Seville and were living in a cramped tourist apartment near the cathedral, we used to lie in bed at night listening to the buzz of voices rising from the café-bars that lined our street. At first I desperately wished that everyone would go home and let me sleep in peace. But I gradually got used to it, then began to find it deeply soothing, a kind of cheery white noise that reminded me that for tonight, at least, all was well with the world outside my doorstep.

Until a few months ago, I would have said there was no word to describe this lovely sensation, but then I stumbled upon the *Dictionary of*

Obscure Sorrows, which defines emotions we all feel but don't have the words to express. My favorite entry reads, "Midding: feeling the tranquil pleasure of being near a gathering but not quite in it — hovering on the perimeter of a campfire, chatting outside a party while others dance inside, resting your head in the backseat of a car listening to your friends chatting up front — feeling blissfully invisible yet still fully included, safe in the knowledge that everyone is together and everyone is okay, with all the thrill of being there without the burden of having to be."

And that, perhaps, is one of the best thing that Seville can offer us, the kind of café-bar where even a foreigner crossing its threshold for the first time can slip into that comforting sense of midding.

The foodie revolution

To those raised on the solid bedrock of old-school cooking, Seville's recent foodie revolution couldn't have been more shocking if it had arrived in the city by flying saucer. Seemingly overnight we had Thai food, Peruvian-Japanese restaurants, Mexican taquerias, vegan fare, organic chorizo, and impossible-to-define fusion places with amusing light fixtures and bewildering menus. The creativity of the menus, quality of the food, and cleverness of décor is gobsmacking; even if you aren't active on social media you'll find yourself reaching for your phone's camera. Rich and I cheerfully paid the higher prices and even put up with the inconvenience of having to make reservations, which until two years ago was rarely necessary except for large groups or high-end places like the Hotel Alphonse XIII.

Not all the gourmet places are new; a few excellent ones — Contenedor, Vineria San Telmo, and Eslava — have been around for years. All the great foodie places below offer outdoor seating, take *reservas* (reservations) online, and have at least some staff who speak English to help with bookings and special requests.

Contenedor, Calle *San Luis 50*, one of the best menus in town

Eslava, *Calle Eslava 3*, cozy, with creative, award-winning tapas

Vineria San Telmo, *Paseo de Catalina de Ribera 4*; great menu and the very best desserts in the city

Bar Castizo, *Calle Zaragoza 6*; good food, unusual domino-decorated walls

Casa Ozama, *Av. de la Borbolla 59*, sumptuous decor, excellent food, quite pricey (for Seville)

Maquiavelo, *Paseo de las Delicias*, the hottest spot with outrageous entertainment

I've been to all of these except Maquiavelo, which I understand is spectacular by the standards of any urban metropolis and particularly stunning to those raised in Seville's more conservative culinary environment. When a couple of Spanish men I know went there recently, one met his friend at the table on the upper floor saying, "I'm not sure this place is for me. There's a guy downstairs playing a piano — and it's on fire!" He meant this literally; apparently there were actual flames erupting from the instrument. He added, "It's just not what I'm used to." Obviously this is a place that merits in-depth, personal research on my part. Watch my blog for updates.

Merienda (afternoon snack)

Alert readers with good math skills will have noticed that so far I've only talked about four meals. In the interests of efficiency, I discussed lunch and dinner together, passing over (for the moment) the delightful post-siesta interlude known as *merienda* (afternoon snack). Let's get to that happy subject now, shall we?

You can enjoy your *merienda* at home or just about any café-bar, especially those listed above as good breakfast choices (except for the XIX, which after breakfast turns into a drinks-only bar). Or you might want to stop in at a bakery where you can sit down and enjoy coffee with pastries or cookies. To be honest, Seville's traditional pastries aren't outstanding; they have a tendency to be bland and sugary rather than flavorful.

For my *merienda* I often have a *torta de aceite* (olive oil cookie), invented here in Seville by Ines Rosales in 1910 and still sold wrapped in old-style waxed paper. In addition to the original *anís*, you can get them in various sweet and savory flavors including orange, cinnamon, and sesame. You'll find them in countless local bakeries and shops, or you can take some home from the Ines Rosales store in Plaza San Francisco.

Other local specialties include *torrijas* (similar to French toast but served cold, bathed in honey), *milihojas de crema*, (flaky pastry filled with whipped cream), spongy little muffins called *magdalenas*, crumbly Christmas cookies known as *polvorones* (literally dusty ones), *yemas* (an insanely sweet candy made of egg yolk and sugar), and *huesos de santo* (bones of the saint, a kind of marzipan stuffed with *yema*). For the feast of the Three Kings, everyone buys *Roscón de Reyes*, a donut-shaped cake stuffed with whipped cream; a single bean is hidden inside for luck. Did I mention Sevillanos have a sweet tooth?

If you're out and about around 5:00 pm, you'll find people gathering at bakeries and cafés all over town. Here are some you might consider.

Pan y Piu, *Calle Cabeza del Rey Don Pedro 15*, the only place I buy bread; indoor only

Los Ángeles, *Calle Adriano 2*, traditional bakery with outdoor tables

Ochoa, *Calle Sierpes 45*, very old school with an attentive staff

Convento del San Leandro, *Plaza de San Ildefonso*, run by cloistered nuns; takeaway only

Full disclosure: the sweets sold at the Convent of Saint Leandro are unremarkable at best, but as a shopping experience it's hard to beat. You step inside a special entrance in the vast cloistered convent, built in 1295, and call out your order to the nun, who is invisible behind a turntable fit into the wall. To observe the strictest form, you begin by saying *"Ave María Purísima,"* (Hail Mary the Pure) to which the nun replies, *"Sin pecado consebido"* (Conceived without sin). And then you place your order. However, most people skip this and just say, *"Media kilo de yemas"* (half a kilo of *yemas*) or whatever else they've chosen from the price list posted on the wall. You put your money on the turntable, and your order and change appear on the next spin of the turntable.

Que le pongo? (What's your drink order?)

Work, play, shopping — it's all thirsty business, and local tavernkeepers are standing by to help. Beer is the beverage of choice, especially during the hot summer months, and it's often ordered at the start of a meal, to quench your thirst and wake up your palate before you settle into a bottle of wine (or more beer). Most places only carry a single brand of beer, which they order by the barrel and sell by the half pint in small glasses. You don't specify a brand, you just ask for a *cerveza* (beer), or the more colloquial *cervecita* (a little beer), or a *caña* (draft). Many places, such as El Tremendo at Calle Felipe 13 and the Bar Jota at Calle Luis Montoto 52, are famous for extra cold beer, and on hot nights the sidewalks around them are jammed with revelers.

Having grown up in California, where wine drinking is taken very seriously indeed, I am always a bit staggered by Seville's casual attitude toward *vino*. Bartenders will ask if you want *blanco* (white) or *tinto* (red). Don't worry if you get flustered and ask for *rojo* (the color red) as they'll still get your drift, but *tinto* is the correct term. You might want to specify Rioja or Ribera del Duero, two of Spain's most famous wine regions and very reliable, especially for reds.

The bartender will then ask if you want *seco* (dry) or *dulce* (sweet) or possibly *afrutado* (fruity). And this is where I run into trouble. I'm a white wine drinker, and what I actually like is a full-bodied, buttery white with a complex flavor and a long finish. I have embarrassed myself and numerous waiters attempting to obtain something — anything — along these lines in Seville. They always listen politely until I run out of words, and then they say, making a massive effort to appease the loony foreigner, "*Así que ... semi-seco?*" (So ...

somewhat dry?)

This can be vexing, as unlike the dependable Spanish *tintos,* the *blancos* vary considerably, from delightful to the kind of stuff they serve out of boxes in American dive bars. So I have devoted many hours of diligent trial and error to the question, and I have figured out my best bet is a Rueda verdejo (Roo-AY-dah vare-DAY-ho). Verdejo is a full-bodied grape that originated in North Africa and arrived in Spain's Rueda region in the 11th century, where it was developed into a dense, sherry-like wine. Then in the 1970s some brilliant, public-spirited winemakers from Rueda and France teamed up to create the fresher verdejo we know today. Whew! I can now order a drinkable *blanco* wherever I go. And so can you.

Hard liquor is considered an after-dinner drink in Seville, and there are lots of *bars de copa* (drinks-only bars) around for this purpose. The most unusual is the Garlochi, Calle Boteros 26, lavishly decorated in a tongue-in-cheek *Semana Santa* theme. Their signature cocktail is *Sangre de Cristo* (Blood of Christ), often served in a chalice. I always tell people it leaves a diabolical hangover, but nobody ever pays any attention. (You have been warned!)

For sheer glamour, it's hard to beat the Bar Americano at the lavish Alfonse XIII Hotel; it's one of the few places around that can make you an American-style dry martini. (Be careful about ordering "a martini" elsewhere, as you may be served a glass of Martini and Rossi vermouth. If you asked for olives in it, the results are pretty ghastly.)

Another great spot for carefully crafted cocktails is a cozier venue near the cathedral called The Second Room, Calle de Placentines 19. Not sure what to order? A local favorite is *gin-tonic* (gin and tonic).

One of the great things about a night on the town in Seville is that you're nearly always close enough to your hotel or Airbnb to walk home, allowing your head to clear and giving you a chance to discuss the evening with your companions and consider what kind of fun you'll organize for the next day

.

6.
WHAT ELSE CAN I DO FOR FUN?

Festivals and dining out loom large on everyone's calendar, of course, but the city offers plenty of other ways to entertain yourself. As of this writing, all Seville's major entertainment and sports venues are open again. Masks are worn in public indoor spaces, such as flamenco *tablaos*, concert halls, churches, and museums, but social distancing is no longer mandatory, and outdoor events, such as *futbol* (soccer) matches, tend to be very crowded indeed.

Futbol (soccer)

Sports enthusiasts (and I confess I'm not one of them, but don't let that stop you) will rejoice to hear the Sevilla Fútbol Club plays nearly all year except July and early August. Check the online schedule and book tickets well in advance if you'd like to see a *partido* (game). Sevilla FC is currently ranked third in the top-level La Liga, and fans sporting their traditional red and white colors can be seen streaming to at-home games in the Ramón Sánchez Pizjuán Stadium in the Nervión district and crowding the city's bars when they play away.

Sevilla FC was founded in 1907 by the city's aristocratic families, and other segments of society, annoyed at being excluded, formed their own team two years later, launching a rivalry that's lasted more than a century. The second club's official name Real Betis Balompié, better known simply as Betis, from the old Roman name for the Guadalquivir River. Currently ranked 6th in La Liga, their tumultuous history includes great victories, bitter defeats, and passionate loyalty, embodied in their slogan, *¡Viva el Betis manque (aunque) pierda!* (Long live Betis even when they lose!). The team plays in the Estadio Benito Villamarín in the southern section of the city, and you'll see their official colors of green and white displayed in blue-collar bars everywhere. Fierce loyalty to one or the other team is a hallmark of Sevillano life.

Flamenco

My preferred form of entertainment is flamenco, the passionate dance that originated here in southern Spain, a mix of local folkloric dance and the wilder rhythms of the Romani. Here in its birthplace, you can see some of the best flamenco in the world. Theaters dedicated to flamenco are called *tablaos*, but you'll find performances everywhere: upscale hotels, dinner shows, restaurants, bars, and in the streets for spare change. But the best way to see it is in one of the small, informal venues known as *peñas*, usually found on back streets, with appreciative local audiences, late hours, and a disappointing tendency to close forever the day after you've discovered them. You can Google "*flamenco peña Sevilla*" and try your luck.

Unless I have discovered a promising new *peña*, I usually take my friends to the intimate Casa de la Guitarra at Calle Masón del Moro 12, near the cathedral. Although you can book online, I always go in person so I can request seats in the first row; you really want a good view of the fancy footwork. This is also a good opportunity to take my friends inside while the space is empty so I can show them the dozens of guitars lining the walls, a collection assembled by the owner, award-winning flamenco guitarist José Luis Postigo.

Flamenco shows are fun and colorful, and the *toque* (guitar playing) and *baile* (dance) are always crowd pleasers. The *cante flamenco* (flamenco singing), however, is an acquired taste. It has a wailing quality to it, much like Arabic songs only raspier; if it's too melodic, aficionados say it's been compromised to satisfy mainstream musical tastes. The words are usually so drawn out that it's impossible to understand their meaning, but you can be sure the themes are much like the American blues: lost loves, nostalgia for home, luck going from bad to worse. I've learned to love the *cante flamenco*, but don't be surprised if you find it tough going at first.

I've known quite a few flamenco dancers, students and professionals, and been to my share of shows, and without doubt best performance I've seen was by the notorious dancer Farroquito. I first saw him in 2004 when Spanish friends suggested stopping for a nightcap at Bar Plata (across from the Macarena Church). Arriving around midnight, when Seville's social life is generally hitting its stride, we were surprised to discover the place was deserted. We had just settled at a table with our drinks when the door opened and five young Romani men strolled in.

My friend's eyes widened and she leaned forward, whispering, "That's Farruquito!" She indicated a boy of 22, very slim, with long black hair and fine-boned features. "The best flamenco dancer of his generation. They say –" Here she dropped her voice even lower. "They say he killed a man in a hit-and-run accident, and he tried to tell people his younger brother was driving, because he knew the boy was too young to be sent to prison. The case is about to go to trial."

Farruquito and his friends collected their drinks and sat at a table in the corner, talking and laughing. Occasionally they broke out into a bit of flamenco singing, their hands clapping out the complicated rhythms, boot heels tapping the floor. It may have been Farroquito's last night on the town for a while. Nobody believed the kid brother story (I later learned it was actually a young cousin in the car), and the dancer was soon convicted and sent to jail. Ten years later I was having coffee in Bar Alfalfa when my idle glance fell on a poster advertising an upcoming show by Farroquito. He'd served his time, been out for a while, and was performing in a downtown concert hall the next night. Did I go? Of course!

Farruquito was easily the best dancer I've ever seen, quick and graceful, his feet moving so fast they became a blur. His home town crowd had come to cheer him on: portly men in flashy suits, lithe young women who moved like dancers, older women with magnificent hair and tight leopard print dresses, young boys looking nervous and ill-at ease in stiff suit jackets, and characters I'd seen hanging around the local cafés and flamenco bars for years. At the end of the performance, Farruquito invited the boys up on to the stage to show off their dance skills, and these young students did him proud, their moves strong and graceful, their faces alight with joy and terror.

The plump, middle-aged woman next to me shouted and clapped

and half-leapt out of her seat at peak moments of the show. After the curtain fell and the tumultuous applause finally died down, she turned to me and said, "I am the happiest woman in the world."

Not all flamenco shows are quite that thrilling, but they offer good entertainment and most of my visitors are only too happy to attend one while they're in Seville. Asking whether they want to go to a bullfight is another matter entirely.

Bullfights

Like *cante flamenco*, bullfights are an acquired taste. To most Americans they're as grotesque and barbaric as ancient Roman gladiatorial death matches and should be permanently outlawed on humanitarian grounds. And who can say they're wrong? I felt that way too, at first. I've never become a fan, but over the years, I've learned to respect the role bullfights play in Seville's culture: a nod to the ancient bull-worshiping cults, held in bullrings modeled on Roman coliseums, and still viewed as the ultimate test of bravery, skill, and art. Sevillanos take great pride in holding the nation's most prestigious events in the Plaza de Toros de la Real Maestranza de Caballería de Sevilla, better known as the Maestranza.

The season begins on Easter Sunday (April 17 in 2022), runs into early summer, pauses during the crushing heat of July and August, then continues in September and early October. If you're not up for an actual bullfight (and who could blame you?), you might want to take the Maestranza bullring tour, which includes the chapel (where some very serious praying goes on, as you can imagine) and the entrance through which the *toreros* (as bullfighters are called here) arrive clad in their spangly *trajes de luces* (suits of lights), while crowds of fans line the way and cheer as if they were rock stars.

Every tour guide has favorite stories to share, and the first time I went, I was lucky enough to be told about the famous mother of a notorious bull. "This is Islera," said my guide, in the tone of profound loathing usually reserved for mentioning Hitler or Vlad the Impaler. "The bull that killed the great *torero* Manolete in 1947. Islera was, of course, killed. And afterwards, they went and found his mother and killed her too, so that she never again produced another murderer." Now does that seem sporting? I ask you!

Of course, *futbol* matches, bullfights, and flamenco shows are only the tip of the entertainment iceberg. The city enjoys plenty of live music, from rock to classical to blues to jazz to cutting-edge stuff that's way above my pay grade, as well as opera, ballet, theater, comedy, and other performing arts. The Mueso de Bellas Artes (Fine Arts Museum) has a large collection of paintings, including such local favorites such as

)usly attired saints of Francisco de Zurbarán, the rosy Virgins ~. ₋₋₋₋₋₋₋₋₋₋₋ Esteban Murillo, and Valdés Leal's grotesque cherubs, which to me are the stuff of nightmares but are much admired around here. To each their own!

Excursions outside the city

One thing that's popular with just about everybody around here is a good road trip. There are countless charming villages and dramatic monuments easily accessible by car, bus, or train. I like public transit, which is convenient to most places, inexpensive, better for the environment, and less stressful than driving, parking, and worrying about where you left your vehicle several hours and glasses of wine ago. But that's me. If you want to hire a car, there's a cluster of rental agencies around Seville's Santa Justa Railway Station, so you can pick up and return the car without ever having to navigate the labyrinthine streets of the city center.

I often take visitors out by bus to see the ancient Roman city of Italica, six miles northwest of Seville. The first Roman settlement in Spain and the first Roman city outside of Italy, it was built to house veterans of military campaigns. Italica was the birthplace of Roman Emperors Trajan and Hadrian, who poured in money into the town, building homes with lovely mosaic floors (many still in place and on display) and public works including a massive amphitheater that once enabled 25,000 bloodthirsty spectators to watch gladiators fight to the death.

When I took my sister Kate there, she exclaimed, "Hey, this is the Dragonpit! The actual Dragonpit from *Game of Thrones*!"

If you watched that epic TV series, you may recall this setting, used in the scene where Daenerys "Mother of Dragons" Targaryen arrives on the back of a flying dragon for a showdown with the psychopathic queen Cersei Lannister. Today, even without actual dragons, the ancient Roman gladiator pit is awe-inspiring and well worth a visit.

If you're interested in Roman sites, you'll want to consider a few days in Mérida, a town 119 miles to the north of Seville. Here you can walk across the longest Roman bridge still in existence and admire the Forum, the *Acueducto de los Milagros* (Aqueduct of Miracles), the *Circus Maximus*, two Roman reservoirs still in active use, and the splendid amphitheater and theater complex. The whole area is breathtaking and usually inspires long conversations about how clever those Roman engineers were, to do all this without computer imaging, using only the kinds of hand tools (hammer, pick, chisel, manual drill, etc.) most guys have in their man cave back home. It's rather humbling.

If you prefer medieval sites to Roman ruins, consider Aracena, just 56 miles from Seville. It's scarcely more than a village, with just 8000 inhabitants clustered around the 13th century castle and the Priory Church, which back in the day belonged to the Knights Templar.

Possibly the most romanticized figures in the Crusades, the Knights Templar were founded in 1118, blessed by the Pope, and famed for their battlefield prowess. Less visibly, the 90% of the order who were non-combatants worked in finance, establishing a large economic infrastructure throughout Christendom, which many consider the forerunner of modern banking and possibly the world's first multinational corporation. Eventually their wealth and power alarmed the Pope and then the King of France, where the order was centered. In 1307 King Philip IV (who was deeply in debt to the order) organized a massive, one-day attack on all Templars in France, seizing their assets and burning many at the stake. Rumor has it that a remnant of the Templars still exists, and that a secret chamber behind the altar in Aracena's Priory Church is reserved for their clandestine use.

But to me Aracena's most impressive attraction lies beneath the castle and the church: the *Gruta de las Maravillas* (Grotto of Marvels), a vast underground cave with twisting passages, strange mineral formations, and several lakes. Fans of the original 1959 film may recognize the caverns as the setting for some of the most dramatic scenes in *Journey to the Center of the Earth.*

The town also boasts a branch of the famous Museo de Jamón (ham museum), a collection so vast it is housed in sites throughout Spain. The first one I saw was in Madrid, and I was astonished by the number and variety of ham legs I glimpsed through the window. Naturally I convinced Rich we had to go in and investigate further. The good news: there was no admission fee. The bad: it's actually just a ham store with a clever name.

Seville and the surrounding region have much to offer visitors. So far I've been concentrating on the major points of interest, but I think we know each other well enough by now that I can suggest a little walk on the wilder side, through the strange and mysterious world of Seville's tall tales and superstitions.

7.
WHAT'S WITH ALL THE ODDBALL MYTHS & LEGENDS?

As a child, I loved a line from *Through the Looking Glass* (the sequel to *Alice's Adventures in Wonderland*) that follows Alice's remark, "One can't believe impossible things."

"I daresay you haven't had much practice," replied the Queen. "When I was your age, I always did it for half-an-hour a day. Why, sometimes I've believed as many as six impossible things before breakfast."

That Queen would have felt right at home in Seville, where my credulity is constantly strained — and my funny bone tickled — by the myths and legends people have passed on to me as gospel truth. Here are some of my favorite impossible stories, and I hope you'll manage to swallow at least six of them before breakfast.

Pedro the Cruel nailed his own head to the wall. One dark night in the fourteenth century, young King Pedro the Cruel ("Pedro the Just" to his friends) was waylaid on a back street in my neighborhood. He himself had outlawed dueling, but his opponent, a young aristocrat with a political chip on his shoulder, gave him no choice but to defend himself. The clash of swords caused an old woman to lean out of an upstairs window with a lantern to see what was going on. She was so alarmed by the fight below that she dropped the lantern, startling both men and giving the king his opportunity to make the fatal thrust. Leaving his attacker's corpse on the sidewalk, the king slipped away into the darkness as quietly as he could. However, the old woman heard the telltale creak of his knee from an old injury, a sound familiar to everyone in the city.

The dead youth's family showed up at the Alcázar palace demanding the killer be found and brought to justice. The king, thinking no one knew the truth, promised a hefty sum of gold as a reward, and the old woman's son — who by now had heard the whole story from his mother — came to claim it. But he was far too clever to do so directly. He took the king aside, pretending to point out the culprit from the window, but actually gesturing to a small mirror on the wall. The king turned around and said, "Good news, my lords! We know who has done this dastardly deed. Give this man the reward!" The old woman's son took the money and slipped prudently away.

"This foul deed will not go unavenged," declared the king. "Tomorrow, I will nail the head of the killer to the wall at the scene of the crime." This grisly custom was common in those days, and naturally everyone in the city showed up, agog to know whodunnit. The king arrived leading a donkey on whose back was a large box. "The killer's head is inside this box," he told the assembled crowd. "But to reveal his identity would be to spark a feud that would have the streets of this city running with blood. I am responsible for keeping the peace. Therefore I am nailing this head to the wall inside this box, securing it with iron bands, and posting a guard on it day and night. I want no more bloodshed in Seville!"

And so matters stood for some years. Eventually the king was killed by his illegitimate half-brother, who from then on was known as Enrique el Fratracida (Henry the Brother-Slayer). One of Enrique's first acts was dispatching men to wall in order to take down the box and find out what was inside. They found a marble bust of Pedro's head. It's still on that wall (without the box) on Calle Cabeza del Rey Don Pedro (Head of King Pedro Street).

Doña María Coronel's body is miraculously preserved. Doña

María Coronel's "miraculously preserved" corpse is quite shriveled and mummified, although the fact it hasn't turned to dust after five centuries is something of a marvel. And it's actually a blessing we can't see her features too clearly, as she was famously disfigured in a gruesome encounter with our old friend, Pedro the Cruel.

The moment he saw María's lovely face, Pedro became infatuated. The pesky problem of a devoted, wealthy, powerful husband was soon solved; Pedro dispatched him to a dangerous battlefield and made María a widow. After that Pedro chased her all over the city for months. She frequently took refuge in a convent with sympathetic nuns, and once, they say, she lay down in the convent's garden while plants miraculously grew over her, hiding her from the King's sight.

Eventually Pedro managed to corner María in the convent kitchen and it was there she took her stand. (Brace yourself; here comes the grisly part.) As he advanced upon her, she picked up a pan of boiling oil and threw it in her own face. The damage was horrific and the king, aghast at this turn of events, paid lavishly for the nuns to nurse her back to health. Incredibly María not only survived but went on to found the Santa Inéz Convent, where she lived to the age of 77. On the anniversary of her death, December 2, and occasionally at other times, her distinctly creepy remains are put on display in the chapel at her convent on Calle

Doña María Cornel Street.

Hercules founded Seville. Having your city established by an actual god conveys certain bragging rights, and to make certain nobody missed this point, in 1574 city officials built a vast public garden — Europe's first — and named it the Alameda de Hercules. For decoration they chose six Roman columns that had stood on the other side of town for 14 centuries. Hauling ancient, 30-foot stone columns in wooden wagons over unpaved streets through a busy city; what could possibly go wrong? Incredibly, two made it safely to the new garden before one managed to roll off and shatter spectacularly in the faces of horrified onlookers.

No doubt a few heads rolled — possibly literally — over that snafu, and suddenly no one wanted the job of pillar transporter. The two surviving columns, topped with statues of Hercules and Julius Cesar respectively, stand at the southern end of the Alameda, their off-center alignment reflecting space left for the third that never arrived. The other three columns are aging gracefully in the Calle Mármoles (Marbles Street), where they are likely to remain until the end of time.

A crocodile was sent to woo a Spanish princess. In 1260 the Sultan of Egypt sent a delegation laden with exotic gifts to ask for the hand of Princess Berenguela, daughter of King Alfonso X. The gifts included a live crocodile, a domesticated giraffe, an elephant tusk, and a wizard's wand. (I know, right? And nowadays guys get away with bringing us flowers and chocolates!) The king rejected the proposal but kept the gifts; the crocodile, in particular, thrilled the populace for years.

When the beast had breathed its last, the king had its body stuffed and hung up in the cathedral along with the tusk, the wand, and the giraffe's bridle bit. When the crocodile's body eventually crumbled, a wooden replica was hung in its place, where it remains today, on the ceiling by the exit onto the Patio de los Naranjos (Patio of the Orange Trees).

A murder inspired the "Puppy" statue of Jesus. "This statue was modeled after a man known as *El Cachorro* in 1682," a Spanish friend told me. We were standing before the carved wooden image of Christ on the cross, head thrown back, eyes looking to heaven. The official name is *Cristo de la Expiracion* (Expiring Christ) but everyone calls the image *El Cachorro*, which means The Puppy, possibly a reference to the model's reputation as a bit of a hound dog.

They say the model was a handsome young Romani who was coming home from a tryst with a noble married lady when her husband caught up with him on the Isabel II Bridge (better known as the Triana Bridge). Some claim the woman's lover was really El Cachorro's bastard brother, and it was all a terrible mistake. Be that as it may, the husband ran the fellow through with his sword just as sculptor Francisco Ruiz de Gijón happened to pass by. He'd spent the night roaming the city's streets in search of inspiration for the statue of Christ he'd been commissioned to carve. Seeing *El Cachorro* (or his bastard brother) breathe his last, the sculptor knew he had found the perfect image. *El Cachorro* is one of the highlights of *Semana Santa*, and during the off season, he can be viewed in the Basílica del Cristo de la Expiración on Calle Castilla in Triana.

Sister Angela of the Cross is miraculously preserved in death. While the other two famous "miraculously preserved bodies" in Seville — Doña María Coronel and San Fernando, the king who reclaimed Seville for Spain — only appear on rare occasions, the mortal remains of Seville's most recent saint are on permanent display. Saint Angela of the Cross was canonized in 2003 for her good works caring for the city's poor, ill, and disadvantaged. Born in 1846, she grew up so sickly she was deemed unfit for religious life. Having been rejected by several convents, she started one of her own and ran it until 1932, when she died at the age of 86.

There's lots of speculation about what they did to preserve her body, because she appears plump, rosy, and bursting with health in the glass case under the altar in the chapel of her convent. You can visit her there, in the Instituto de las Hermanas de la Cruz (Sisters of the Company of the Cross) on Calle Santa Angela 4. A life-sized statue of the nun stands in front of the convent, and there are nearly always fresh flowers at her feet, left by the faithful.

The Purgatory tiles predict your matrimonial prospects. Just a stone's throw from Saint Angela's statue you'll find the church San Pedro, which has some rather unusual artwork on its outside wall: ceramic tiles depicting Purgatory, the place traditional Catholics believe they'll be sent to atone for their sins before ascending to heaven. Set in an elaborate Baroque border, it shows a group of naked people, looking bored and slightly peeved, standing in the midst of burning flames; angels are grabbing those who have served their time and hauling them upward toward Jesus and a gathering of saints. It's a lot to take in. But wait, there's more.

"Can you find the bird?" asked the Spanish friend who'd brought me there to see it. She told me the artist was Juan Oliver (apparently no relation to John Oliver of the *Last Week Tonight* TV show) who always hid a bird somewhere in his artwork. "If you find this one," she told me, "they say you'll be married within the year." This feature wasn't particularly useful to me after decades of married life, but lots of my friends and visitors spend time intently studying the tiles. And let me just say finding that bird is harder than you'd think. If you'd like to try it, go to my website (EnjoyLivingAbroad.com) and search for Purgatory tiles. You'll find an image of the whole piece and, if necessary, a link to the detail of the bird.

The Shoemaker's Tomb also foretells wedding bells. Didn't find the bird on your own? Not to worry, there's another church where you can hedge your matrimonial bets: the magnificent old Santa Ana church across the river in the Triana district. A tomb built into an interior wall is said to be the final resting place of an African shoemaker. For reasons nobody can quite remember now, it's believed that if you touch this tomb with the toe of your shoe, you'll be married within the year. Needless to say the wall has been battered to bits by centuries of hopefuls. Eventually the priests got tired of replacing the tiles and put up an iron railing — but positioned it just close enough that if you really stretch, your shoe can nudge the side of the tomb.

The Science Museum will give you the shivers. OK, this isn't actually part of any myth or legend, but while we're visiting the city's oddball side, I just had to mention the quirky little museum called La Casa del Ciencia (The House of Science). You'll find it inside the dramatic 1929 Peruvian Pavilion in Parque María Luisa. Part mad scientist's laboratory and part animal morgue, it displays glass jars of bats and other beasts, a rare Iberian lynx with his eyes sewn shut, and various large birds laid on slabs with old-style mortuary toe tags tied to their feet with string. It makes a pleasantly macabre little side trip when visiting the Plaza de España.

I've been exploring Seville since 2001, and I'm still discovering new dark corners and tall tales. Not everyone finds these stories completely plausible, and I've often been questioned about the details, especially the bits of dialogue I quote from Pedro the Cruel. But accuracy isn't the point; these stories have been passed on by word of mouth for generations because everyone loves the drama they add to the streets, bridges, and buildings that make up the landscape of our lives. Even if you're just visiting for a short while, these stories will enrich your view of the city and leave you with a better understanding of the character of the Sevillano people.

8.
PEOPLE STILL TAKE SIESTAS?
DO I HAVE TO?

Yes, many people in Seville still take daily siestas, although younger

business people often don't, and there's pressure from the European

Union to disband the practice and get everyone on the same hours.

Madrid is gradually complying, but Seville, to a large extent, is holding

firm. Except for the major shops downtown, just about everything closes

for several hours at midday, usually from 2:00 to 5:00, so people can

enjoy a leisurely lunch and a little siesta, followed by coffee and

marienda (afternoon snack). They then return to work until 8:00 or 9:00

o'clock.

And no, of course you don't have to take an afternoon nap. But

as my reader Scott commented recently, "I would say the siesta and

teatime are the two most civilized things to come out of [Western culture]." Well said, sir! Here in Seville we call it *marienda* instead of teatime, but the idea is the same. Life is more gracious when you don't view it as a day-long marathon but instead take time to rest and regroup in the afternoon — especially when you're coping with stupefying heat of Seville's summer.

Yet there are always skeptics, who ask in scandalized tones, "Why waste the best part of the day sleeping when you could be out looking at monuments and taking Instagram photos?"

When my American visitors hear that I actually take time out every afternoon for a siesta, they often look at me sideways, obviously wondering if I've entered my dotage, never matured past the age of five, or deteriorated into a day-drinking couch potato during the pandemic.

Some sidle away in quiet alarm at this point, but the hardier souls ask, "You take a nap every afternoon? Really? But then how can you sleep at night?"

"I sleep better at night when I take a siesta," I explain. "I'm a more relaxed person. My days have a gentler rhythm. And it's like having fourteen mornings a week!"

If they're still unconvinced, I can now point out that Spain was just awarded the highest health grade on the planet in a sleep study comparing life expectancy, the Bloomberg Healthiest Country Index, and average sleep time. "Bloomberg gave Spain the highest health grade: 93 percent (that's a solid A), while the U.S. came in 35th with a score of 73 (eek, that's a D...minus)," reported the online magazine *Well + Good.* You may be surprised to learn more snooze time doesn't automatically earn a higher health grade. Spain averages a modest 7 hours and 10 minutes, while Mexico, despite a solid 9 hours nightly, has the lowest life expectancy of the 37 countries in the study.

Lots of factors influence Spain's health grade, of course, including universal access to free medical care and the famous Mediterranean diet. But I am convinced (based on completely random, unscientific, anecdotal evidence) that another key element is their relaxed attitude toward sleep.

As far as I can tell, nobody here in Seville worries much about how many hours of shut-eye they're getting. In the US, we're bombarded with articles such as the CDC's "1 in 3 adults don't get enough sleep" with the ominous subhead, "A good night's sleep is critical for good health" and an opening sentence citing the Morbidity and Mortality Weekly Report. Good grief! One minute into the article and I'm already feeling doomed.

When I moved to Seville, I was staggered by everyone's insouciant attitude toward sleep. Last night, for instance, a casual dinner with friends lasted until 1:30 am — on a Monday. You get even less snooze time during the *Feria de Abril*; many Sevillanos average two hours sleep a night. "It's just a week," they say with a shrug. "I'll be fine." And so they are. Although to be honest, I wouldn't schedule elective surgery, car repair, or a haircut that week. Not everyone will be operating at peak efficiency.

A few years ago, rocket scientists started putting the siesta under a microscope to see if it might prove useful in outer space. "NASA's research showed that naps really can fully restore cognitive function at the same rate as a full night's sleep," reported *Business Insider*. "The space agency found that pilots who slept in the cockpit for 26 minutes showed alertness improvements up to 54% and job performance improvements by 34%." Astronauts call this a NASA nap.

In business circles, the preferred term is power nap, to make it sound more grown-up, professional, and goal-oriented. Executive nappers like to point out how many success icons, such as Winston Churchill, Margaret Thatcher, and Albert Einstein, snoozed every afternoon. They'll then cite the health benefits: siestas reduce the chance of a fatal heart attack by 37% and can reverse information overload and prevent burnout. It's not difficult to do a cost-benefit analysis that favors siestas. Sorry, I mean power naps.

And then there's the coffee nap. I personally have not tried this, but apparently you begin your rest period by downing a latte or espresso, then immediately lie down to sleep or just relax for 20 minutes. Meanwhile, the caffeine molecules are fitting themselves into receptors in the brain that are normally occupied by a chemical called adenosine, which tends to build up during the day, making you sleepy. By around the 20-minute mark, stimulating caffeine molecules have replaced all the sleepy adenosine molecules, leaving you feeling bright-eyed, bushy-tailed, and zippity doo dah. Proponents rave about the reinvigorating effects of this process, which has been dubbed the nappuccino.

Of course, it can be tough to find a suitable spot for a doze, especially if you're traveling or working in a busy office far from your apartment. That's why humanitarians in Barcelona, Spain created Nappuccino Corner, a café where, for the price of a modest lunch with coffee, you get a free siesta in one of their individual resting pods. "They are not completely closed in order to prevent any claustrophobic feeling," says the website, although I suspect it's mostly to prevent any shenanigans from taking place inside.

Seville hasn't installed nappuccino pods in any cafés yet (that I know of) but watch my blog for updates.

With or without coffee, a siesta should only last about 20

minutes. That's because you want to stop before reaching deep REM sleep, which can leave you groggy afterwards. To avoid this, Einstein used to nap with a pencil loosely clasped in one hand, knowing that when he edged toward more profound slumber, the pencil would fall to the floor with a clatter and wake him. Even if you don't sleep but simply rest for 20 minutes, you get the benefits of a siesta. Afterwards, the Spanish advise reanimating yourself with a *marienda* of coffee and sweet pastry — and why not?

Afternoon siestas not only improve your mental and physical wellbeing, they give you something pleasurable to look forward to every day. I begin by closing the shutters to create a cozy twilight, then stretch out on the couch; if it's cool enough, I wrap up in a soft, fuzzy blanket. I open my Kindle, read a few pages, then close my eyes, just for a moment … and wake up twenty minutes or so later, feeling deeply refreshed.

Do siestas really make you healthy, wealthy, and wise? Science says yes, but don't take my word for it, or even Einstein's. Try it for yourself. This will, of course, be easier if you work at home or happen to be in Spain, where everything shuts down for the midday break. And no doubt you're thinking you don't have time, because your schedule is pretty full already. But hey, if Churchill could squeeze in daily naps while fighting Hitler, maybe you can find twenty spare minutes in your schedule, too. Just be prepared for a few quizzical looks from friends, neighbors, and co-workers who have yet to discover the happy truth: taking a siesta is hitting the reset button on your day. And who doesn't want to do that?

And while we're on the subject of local customs, I want to mention another one you may be wondering about: cheek kissing.

Kissing on both cheeks

I was startled to learn, when I first arrived in Seville twenty years ago, that I was expected to kiss just about everybody on both cheeks. My landlady kissed me each time she collected the rent, my banker kissed me after we opened our account, and the flamenco singers in the dubious bar across the street kissed me whenever I dropped in to listen to the music.

After a few awkward fumbles, I learned it was always your right cheek to their right cheek, then you do the left cheeks, and that's it. You never kiss just once (American-style) or do it three times (as in Egypt, Russia, Switzerland, Belgium, and parts of France), or go for four or more, because honestly, who has the time? It can take considerable persistence and agility to dole out *dos besos* (two kisses) to everyone you know when you meet up at a chaotic bar or crowded party. If you miss anybody, it's viewed as a hurtful slight that requires a lengthy and sincere apology, if not outright groveling. In ordinary times, you're wise to kiss first and take names later.

The *dos besos* tradition was largely suspended during the pandemic, and when I returned to Seville in September of 2021, most of my friends, both local and international, bumped elbows and made jokes to get through the slight awkwardness we felt at adopting this new ritual. By October, good friends were starting to lean in for the *dos besos* again, although mostly with careful air kisses rather than actual physical contact; when Omicron hit, that stopped abruptly. Now some people are starting to hug and air kiss both cheeks again, and if the numbers keep dropping, I'll expect a resurgence of full-on, city-wide double kisses. Both the Sevillanos and the expat community remain more circumspect with out-of-town visitors and people they've just met, and hand-shaking has become much more common in those situations. If you want to maintain as much social distance as possible, be prepared to extend your hand or point an elbow at anyone who shows an inclination to move in close.

Kissing, like wine, is designed to smooth the sharper edges of life. It lets us relax and feel connected. Of course, you can't run around doing it just anywhere. Long before Covid, I found that my fellow Californians tend to look at me very oddly indeed if I kiss them the first time we meet. And that goes double in the UK.

Which is why I love the story of Winston Churchill preparing for an especially tricky meeting with French President Charles de Gaulle in 1942.

A diplomatic advisor urged the Prime Minister to treat de Gaulle with kid gloves, adding, "He will probably expect to kiss you on both cheeks."

To which Churchill replied, "All right, all right. I'll be good. I'll be sweet. I'll kiss him on both cheeks — or all four if you'd prefer it."

Luckily for all of us, the idea of kissing on all four cheeks has never really caught on. The *dos besos* tradition, however, is as firmly entrenched in the Spanish psyche as the siesta, and I believe we can expect both customs to remain part of Seville's social landscape for the foreseeable future.

9.
WHAT IF I GET SICK?

Spain's health care system is consistently rated among the best in the world. Right now it holds the rank of eighth best, comparing favorably to the UK (tenth) and the US (an underwhelming thirtieth). So if something (God forbid, touch wood) should ever happen while you're in Seville (which it won't!), you're in excellent hands.

Spaniards, quite rightly, think very highly of their health system and have embraced Covid vaccines as the lifesavers they are. More than 90% of residents over the age of 11 are double vaccinated, and the health system is distributing boosters and injecting kids at an impressive rate.

"Experts attribute Spain's vaccine success, in part, to its widely trusted public health system, which spearheaded the effort," writes Nicholas Casey, Madrid bureau chief of the *NY Times*. "Politicians also played a big role, taking their doses with fanfare early on and avoiding politicized debate about the vaccine. Spaniards, for the most part, followed the health guidance of their leaders when it came to vaccines, masks and other precautions." Salvador Illa, who oversaw the first year of Spain's pandemic response, observes, "As far as vaccines go, in Spain there's just a wide consensus among citizens — they follow the recommendations of the scientists."

Wow. Confidence in the public health system. Leaders avoiding controversy. Trust in science. What a country!

Finding masks and tests

Despite the high vaccination rate, people here still take Covid seriously, knowing that breakthrough cases are common. In fact, nearly every household I know has had at least one member contract the virus, sometimes with quite serious results, although most caught the milder Omicron version. Everyone is completely matter-of-fact about wearing masks in all indoor public settings and many continue wearing them on the more crowded city streets as well, to be extra cautious.

Should you happen to run short of masks during your stay, they are readily available throughout the city. The most common type is FFP2, similar to the KN95s sold in the US; surgical masks and cloth masks are also available, although they are increasingly less popular as they are known to be less effective. Many souvenir shops sell FFP2s in a variety of cheerful colors and patterns for days when you're in the mood for something jazzier, or you can pick up plain ones at any pharmacy and even some supermarkets.

Depending on current regulations, chances are you'll need a professional Covid test to return to your home country or continue on to your next destination. Google "Covid Test Seville" to find the closest clinic, confirm it does the kind of testing you need in the required timeframe, and book your appointment online. There are dedicated testing sites at the airport, near the railway station, and at multiple locations around town. Friends and relatives recommend Eurofins Megalab (Calle Jesús Del Gran Poder 19, Portal 3) and Synlab (Jose Laguillo 29, near the Santa Justa train station).

If you're here for a longer stay, consider having a Covid test 14 days prior to your departure, just in case you acquired an asymptomatic case of the virus. You don't want to be surprised by this news the day before your flight home. If you test positive two weeks before your departure date, you'll have time to document your recovery. You'll need a copy of your positive viral test result, dated no more than 90 days before the flight's departure, and a letter from a licensed healthcare provider or a public health official stating that you are cleared to travel. This meets current requirements for reentry into the USA, but of course, regulations may change; check the CDC's Covid page and/or other government sites for updates.

Home tests are not accepted by the airlines or government authorities but are very useful for giving you a heads-up about your Covid status so you can either breathe a sigh of relief of quickly adjust plans for your immediate future. Kits are available at any pharmacy; ask for "Covid test" (an English phrase all pharmacists now understand) and expect to pay between 3.5€ and 7€ ($4 and $8).

There was a brief shortage of test kits before Christmas, when everyone in town was self-testing like mad before and after parties and family gatherings. This put me in a bit of a pickle, as I'd asked my 17 guests to self-test (twice, if possible) before coming to lunch on December 25. Our guests wrote to say they'd be happy to test if only they could find the kits. Rich and I had ten kits on hand already and began scouring the city for more. We finally found one pharmacy that had just gotten in a shipment but would only sell us five, leaving us still short of the number needed to have every guest self-test even once. After buying our allotted five, we continued our quest unsuccessfully for hours. And then I had my brilliant idea.

"Go back to where we bought those five tests," I said.

"But they'll recognize me," he objected.

"Not if you're in disguise."

So Rich put on a different jacket, a baseball cap in lieu of his trademark fedora, his other glasses, and my red scarf — and walked out of that pharmacy with five more test kits. He is still basking in the glow of carrying off a successful clandestine mission. Over the next few days, major shipments of kits were delivered throughout Seville, and they've been plentiful in the city's pharmacies ever since.

Pharmacies

Here in Seville, pharmacies are often the most practical entry point into the medical system. Spanish pharmacists are highly trained and legally able to dispense advice and many medications that would require a doctor's visit and prescription in the US. For instance, when a friend arrived in Seville with severe back pain, he asked me how to schedule a doctor's visit so he could get a prescription for the prednisone he'd used for this before. Instead I suggested he email his doctor back home to get the precise dosage, then I took him and the email to Farmacia de la Alfalfa (in Plaza de la Alfalfa) where several of the pharmacists speak English. They sold him the prednisone he needed for about 3.85€ ($4.36).

Medical clinics

Not everything can be handled over the counter, of course, and there are times it's necessary and sensible to consult a physician. When that happens, I take my visitors to my own healthcare provider, Sanitas, which has a walk-in clinic called Centro Médico Milenium La Buhaira at Avenida Eduardo Dato 23.

Back in ordinary times, my wait was rarely more than twenty minutes, and sometimes lasted just the five minutes it took them to run my card through the computer system. Now, with the pandemic backlog still clogging the schedule, I hear wait times are longer and visits to specialists are subject to delay unless the issue is urgent. Your best bet is to go early in the morning, as close to opening time (currently 7:30 am) as possible. Mondays are the most crowded as Milenium and many other clinics are closed on weekends.

Here's what to expect: At the Milenium reception desk, you'll be given a number, which will flash on a screen in the waiting room when it's your turn, indicating which consulting room is expecting you. Go to that door, give a courteous tap, and enter, bringing along any family members or friends who may be with you. You don't have to bring an entourage, of course, but here in Spain medicine is viewed as a family affair; it's assumed you'll appreciate the moral support and someone to help you sort out medicines and therapies. As a foreigner, you may also need someone to help with translation. Most doctors in Milenium and some other clinics will know a little English, but you'll want a translator if you don't speak much Spanish, especially if what you have is less obvious than a hacking cough or flaming rash.

The exam is simple; they don't get the nurse in to take vitals or have you undress and get into a gown. You sit in a visitor's chair and explain the problem. If necessary, the doctor may do a brief exam on a table behind a privacy screen and then give you a diagnosis and any written instructions and/or prescriptions. The lack of fuss gets you in and out in record time.

Visits go even faster if you're in the social security system. I once dropped in to see an 87-year-old friend and found her fretting about an earache. I walked five blocks to the nearest public health center and made an appointment for her later that same day. She wouldn't be seeing a doctor she knew, but thanks to the universal medical records system, the one who was available had my friend's complete health history at his fingertips. He peered into my friend's ear and checked her blood pressure, which had been problematic in the past, but was OK now. He tapped a few keys on his computer and told me he'd prescribed a mild pain killer. When I asked what pharmacy he'd sent the prescription to, he looked at me strangely. "All of them," he said. You've got to love the efficiency! And it was all free, of course.

If you happen to be a member of the military (active, retired, or a spouse), you're entitled to medical care at the US Naval Station Rota, 78 miles south of Seville in the province of Cádiz. It's the largest US military base in Spain, mostly US Navy and US Marine Corps, with smaller contingents of US Army and US Air Force personnel. Although I've been on the base lecturing about travel, I've never obtained any health services there, but I'm told it could be an option for those seeking Covid vaccines or booster shots, as well as other medical services.

Andalucía's free Covid insurance

Everyone worries about what might happen if they contract Covid while they're here. In an effort to allay these concerns, Andalucía is offering international visitors free Covid-19 insurance covering doctor and hospital bills, medicines, hotel accommodations during recovery, and more. It's a generous package, and you'll likely be very grateful for it in the unlikely event you need to take advantage of the offer. But be sure to read the fine print carefully.

For a start, the package is only available an add-on to your own trip insurance. Other conditions include requiring you to stay in licensed commercial lodgings, covering repatriation only within Europe, and charging a 100€ deductible. You don't need to sign up in advance, but you might want to check it out before your trip; visit andalucia.org/en/travel-assistance-insurance to get the full details.

Ambulance service (dial 061)

I'm fortunate enough never to have needed hospitalization in Seville (*gracias a Dios*), but living here, I've naturally listened to plenty of stories. Just as with US hospitals, I've heard about the good and the bad. In an emergency, I would have no hesitation about calling an ambulance. Here you dial 061 to get directly to the ambulance service; the general emergency number is 112.

Rich and I also have an app called Emergency Call Anywhere which gets us to an English-speaking dispatcher and provides them with our GPS location. We haven't had to use it for ourselves, but one day we happened to be walking by just as an older gentleman tripped and fell on the sidewalk. In less than a minute Rich was talking with someone who was prepared to send help. Of course, when something like this happens, everyone on the street rushes over, and a local fellow had been even quicker than Rich, so an ambulance was already en route. Still, it was gratifying to know our app worked.

What, me worry?

It's natural to be nervous about health care in a foreign country, and you're wise to be cautious, do your research, and seek the best available care. But don't automatically assume the best care is back home. An American nurse I know got food poisoning in England, and she insisted on immediately flying back to the US rather than getting treatment from local providers. I don't even want to imagine what that flight was like for her, her husband, the flight attendants, and those seated around her.

Why would an intelligent, well-educated medical professional put herself through that kind of unnecessary suffering?

Because she believed the American health care industry, whose marketing arm has spent billions of dollars trying to convince us that they provide the only decent medical care on the planet. We're told from infancy that any health services outside US borders will be so medieval we'll wind up with something worse than whatever we walked in with. When you're dealing with other developed countries, that's sheer malicious nonsense. According to World Population Review, Spain's healthcare system ranks eighth in the world; the US comes in thirtieth. The UK is tenth, suggesting they would have been more than capable of coping with that nurse's case of food poisoning.

If I was seeking long-term care for a complex problem, sure, I'd probably head back to the US, in large part because it's easier to navigate a familiar system in your own language. But I'd try to balance my options, wherever I was. And that goes for dental care, as well.

Dental care

I don't know about you, but I do not enjoy going to the dentist. In fact, I pretty much need a shot of novocaine just to call and make the appointment, especially if I'm trying out a new dental practice. And that goes triple in a foreign country. I'm such a coward that until a few years ago, I'd always managed to be in America when it was time for dental maintenance. But then an American friend visiting Seville had a minor dental emergency, found someone online, and came out saying wonderful things about Pablo López who runs the LÓ Clinic (Calle Feria 1, behind the Setas). Rich went to Pablo for a chipped tooth and was equally impressed. So I grit my teeth and made an appointment for a long-overdue cleaning. And it's a good thing I did; I saw him in February of 2020 and it was quite a while before I was scheduling any more dental visits.

I was astonished at how efficient and painless everything was at the LÓ Clinic. If you've ever suffered through x-rays taken via a series of uncomfortable vinyl-clad carboard inserts jammed into your cheeks, you'll appreciate that I simply rested my chin on a support and the machine rotated around me like something out of *Star Trek*. The cleaning was all done via water pressure, without a single jab to the gums with a sharp metal implement. Before I knew it I was back out on the street with a brighter smile and a couple of complimentary bamboo toothbrushes.

Pablo and his staff speak a little English, and you can always Google a few phrases ahead of time, such as *diente astillado* or *corona suelta* (chipped tooth or loose crown). If you'll be more comfortable with someone who has a fuller grasp of your own language, my friend Paula recommends Dr. Laura Ugarte of Ugarte Dental (Calle Severo Ochoa 7), and my friend Donna likes Clinica Ardila (Calle Zaragoza 46), where two of the dentists, Sofia and Antonio, speak English.

Wherever you go, expect to pay considerably less than you do back home. At my last visit, I paid 50€ ($57) for a teeth cleaning and learned that if I ever need an implant, the cost would be 1100€ ($1260), compared to $4500 in the States. As if all that wasn't cheering enough, I was told I had excellent teeth and could easily get by with just one cleaning a year. I never hear comments like that in my home state of California, where my pearly whites are assessed in comparison to those of movie stars.

Obviously your best move is not to get sick, chip a tooth, or take a header over the handlebars of your bicycle, as my brother did when he hit a pothole coming back from a long ride through the outskirts of Seville. Mike was lucky to walk away with nothing worse than scratches and a scolding from the clinic nurse, who kept saying sternly, "Tienes 70 años" (You are 70), apparently hoping to convince him to act his age. (But what fun is that?) Life is unpredictable, and you never know when you're going to need a little help from the local medical community. I'm not saying Seville's is perfect (what health system is?), but it has helped me and a lot of others I know to survive when we hit the unexpected potholes in the road of life.

10.
WILL I HAVE REVERSE CULTURE SHOCK GOING HOME?

Arriving home after a long journey is a surreal and often disconcerting experience. Sometimes the well-known nooks and crannies of our own home seem subtly altered, the larger landscape feels off-kilter, and approaching loved ones we left behind feels hesitant and awkward, if only for a moment. Observed with fresh eyes, familiar people and places reveal themselves to us in a whole new way. Moreover, the tiny, incremental changes that took place while we were away hit us all at once. Just when we long to wrap a familiar place around us like a favorite old coat, it feels alien, awkward, and ill-fitting, as if it had shrunk several sizes, grown an extra sleeve, and lost all its buttons.

Now is the time for some serious recombobulation. Ideally you've scheduled some downtime following your return, so you don't need to plunge into your whirlwind schedule right away. Eat nourishing food and plenty of chocolate, drink lots of water, have some coffee in the morning and wine at night, sleep at least twice a day, and veg out with books, TV, and music. Repeat as needed.

Resting and ruminating are essential for processing your memories and absorbing the insights you've gained, so that you can carry everything you learned with you as you resume daily life. "Travel," wrote Catharine Hamm in the *LA Times*, "requires you to be braver than you think you are, whether it's for a week or a year, and involves the joy of finding a better, smarter, stronger self that lasts well past the day you put away your suitcase if, indeed, that day ever comes."

Every time I put away my suitcase, I pause for a moment to imagine when I'll use it again. The possibilities are limitless. I have done a great deal of traveling in my life, visiting more than sixty countries, working in six of them, and living abroad for the better part of twenty years. The world is a vast and (much of the time) beautiful place, and every journey is ripe with possibilities. When we're on the road, those possibilities become more visible because we're looking around with wonder and anticipation, but they don't disappear the day the suitcase goes back up in the attic. We bring our fresh eyes with us as we resume our normal rounds, and if we're lucky, on a good day, we'll see our daily life as the adventure it really is.

As the 17th century Japanese poet Matsuo Basho put it, "Every day is a journey, and the journey itself is home."

*Thanks for joining me on this journey
through Seville's new normal.*

*If you enjoyed this book, please consider
leaving a comment on Amazon.*

*For updates on Seville as the situation unfolds,
check out my blog:*

EnjoyLivingAbroad.com

PREVIEW

If you'd like to know more about what it's like to live overseas (because

hey, you never know; maybe someday?) turn the page for a sample from

my book about the transition Rich and I made from semi-rural Ohio to

Seville, Spain.

Dancing in the Fountain: How to Enjoy Living Abroad

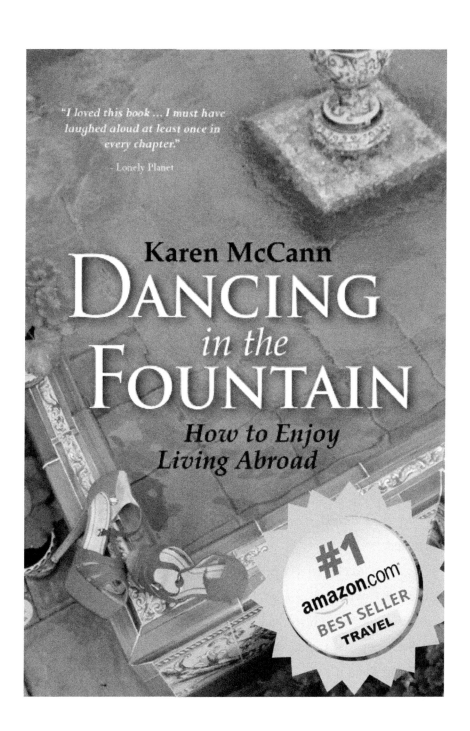

"I loved this book ... I must have laughed aloud at least once in every chapter."

– Lonely Planet

Karen McCann

DANCING
in the
FOUNTAIN

*How to Enjoy
Living Abroad*

#1 amazon.com BEST SELLER TRAVEL

PREFACE

When I was growing up, my friends and I used to ask each other, "If you could live anywhere in the world, where would it be?" We'd then spend hours discussing the rival merits of Paris, London, Rome, and anyplace else we could think of that came under the thrilling and glamorous heading of "abroad." Years later, sitting in a dimly lit San Francisco restaurant on my first date with my husband-to-be, the subject came up again. Rich said, "I'd like to live abroad for a year. What do you think about Singapore?" I knew then that he was a keeper.

As it turned out, instead of Singapore, we went to live in Cleveland.

Two weeks after we came back from our honeymoon in the jungles of Costa Rica, a Cleveland firm made Rich an offer no sane person would have refused, and off we went. My sisters were appalled. Our San Francisco friends started referring to us in the past tense and wondering aloud if we'd done something terrible in a past life to deserve our fate. "Costa Rica?" said an old friend of Rich's. "Cleveland? When are you going to stop testing this woman?"

But as it happened, I loved Cleveland (yes, I did!). I had moved around a lot over the years, propelled by fluctuations in the family fortunes and later my own, and I had learned that I could make a good life for myself practically anywhere. One thing I know to be true: the secret is mentally unpacking your bags. Or, as the Buddhists like to put it, being here now.

In my Cleveland days, "here" was an old stone house on a wooded bluff overlooking a river, and "now" was a life filled with interesting work and great friends. We lived twenty-five miles outside the city, in a semirural area with woods, farms, and a large Amish community. We were deep in the American heartland, about as far from "abroad" as you can get.

But Rich always makes good on his promises, and a mere twenty years later, we moved to southern Spain. It began nearly eleven years ago with a visit to a friend's timeshare on the Mediterranean coast, which led to a return visit the following spring to study Spanish. That's when we took a side trip to Seville and found it too intriguing simply to pass through for a couple of days. We spent four spring vacations in Seville, staying for longer and longer periods, until finally we decided to move there "for a year." We've now been living in Seville for six and a half years, in a slightly crumbling old apartment overlooking the sun-bleached tile roof of an eighteenth-century church. A few years back we sold our beloved Cleveland house and bought a cottage in a small town north of San Francisco, near family and longtime friends, to serve as our home base when we're in the US. But most of our time is spent in Seville, and I'm still astonished at my good fortune.

And here's what I've learned: living abroad is easier than you think.

People often say to me, "You have the best of both worlds."

(Wistful sigh.) "I wish I could do what you do." Half the time, I know perfectly well that my lifestyle wouldn't suit them at all. They've chosen a different path and are just enjoying the kind of fleeting fantasy that comes with reading about people in wildly different circumstances, like Victorian London or outer space, and trying the idea on for size. After a few seconds, they're only too happy to set aside the fantasy to go back to browsing the Kindle store, helping the kids with their homework, or writing an email to colleagues.

But for anyone who might be seriously interested, I'll just say again, it's easier than you think. Of course, moving abroad — or anywhere, for that matter — has its challenges and will take time and effort to plan and carry out. But you don't have to wait until all the stars are aligned, the dog passes away, your grandkids are all happily married with good jobs, and you win the lottery.

Many people are under the impression that living abroad is terribly expensive — and it can be, if you buy a penthouse in the best neighborhood in Paris or Rome. But if you rent a comfortable apartment in a small, affordable city like Seville, your cost of living may actually go down or, as in our case, remain about the same. Although we pay a bit more in airfares every year, our basic expenses (housing, food, clothing, entertainment, ground transportation) are far more modest in Seville than when we made our home in Cleveland. Among other economies, we live in a walking city and don't need a car to get about. Without the car payments, insurance, garage fees, and maintenance, to say nothing of parking tickets, we can easily afford to hop a bus, rent a car, or take a taxi on those rare occasions when we need to.

Moving abroad may not have to wait until you're retired, either. While not every career can be uprooted and taken with you, I have friends in their twenties, thirties, and forties, often with large dogs and/or small children, who have figured out how to work successfully from a foreign base. In these technologically advanced times, all it takes is a computer to manage projects with business associates, keep tabs on investments, and stay in touch with family and friends in other countries. In fact, between Facebook and other media, I am now more familiar with the minutiae of my loved ones' lives than I was when we lived on the same block or even in the same house. And my initial concerns about missing family and friends evaporated when I learned that when you live in a destination city like Seville, *they* come to *you*. Sometimes the biggest challenge is getting them to leave again — but more about that later.

And contrary to what we've all read in so many charming books about Provence and Tuscany, it turns out that when you move to Europe, you are not actually required to purchase a crumbling old farmhouse in the country and spend years restoring it with the help of semiliterate but wise and amusing locals. That's a great life for some, but I find the country and suburbs to be very isolating, especially in a place like southern Spain, where people are slow to befriend anyone they haven't known since baptism. To me, it's infinitely more agreeable to rent an already-restored apartment in the center of a destination city, where the locals are more open to meeting foreigners and there's a lively and diverse international community. During my twenty years in Ohio, I spent more than enough evenings sitting on the back porch listening to the crickets. Now I'm delighted to be able to stroll around the corner to a flamenco show, wine tasting, or concert any night of the week and go out afterwards to a tapas bar with friends.

While you don't have to be wealthy, retired, or willing to restore a crumbling farmhouse to enjoy living abroad, there are some things you *will* need. The first is a good sense of humor, which is essential to surviving the general upheaval of any major life change, and most especially the social and linguistic pratfalls you'll inevitably be taking. Every foreign language is studded with little trip wires, such as the Spanish word *embarazada*, which sounds so much like the English "embarrassed," but in fact means "pregnant," creating endless opportunities for misunderstandings and faux pas. Or there's the common word *huevos*, literally "eggs" but often used as a slang word for testicles. You'll want to be very careful not to ask the guy at the farmers' market whether he has eggs; he'll inevitably reply "Yes, two big ones," and everyone within earshot will fall about laughing until you flee in confusion and have to find someplace else to buy your breakfast groceries.

An adaptable attitude is also a great help when living abroad. Naturally we all make comparisons with our country of origin, but it's best to avoid constantly demanding that other countries measure up to our standards and norms. I recently read a blog called "A Fantasy About Retiring Abroad," in which a financial planner weighed the pros and cons of living in a foreign country. Her conclusion was that it would be utterly impossible for her (and, she implied, anyone with any sense) to live in Europe because the Europeans do not have a "can-do" attitude and frequently fail to meet American efficiency standards. Oh honey, I wanted to tell her, that's the best reason I can think of *for* living in Europe. It's such a relief to live among people who value other things — such as family, friends, slow-cooked meals, witty and intimate conversation — above optimizing time management. It says a lot about our culture that this financial planner couldn't even have a *fantasy* that failed to achieve productivity benchmarks.

Respect for other cultures is essential too. There are times when all of us find it difficult to let go of preconceived notions of how things ought to work, especially in a foreign business setting. As part of our volunteer work for various organizations assisting struggling microenterprises, in the late 1990s Rich and I went to the former Soviet republic of Georgia. At the end of a fat dossier on the company's issues our case manager advised, "Don't write your report on the plane en route to the assignment." He was so right. One of my first suggestions for our clients was a mail marketing campaign. That's when I discovered that the nation's mail system hadn't functioned since the Soviets pulled out.

"Then how do you send out your bills?" I asked.

"We drive to people's homes. And while the bill collector is inside, the driver spray-paints our phone number on the wall of the building."

"And people don't object to that?" I asked incredulously. In the US there would be a lawsuit filed before the paint was dry.

"No, they like having the number handy." Apparently the phone books and directory assistance service had gone the way of the mail system.

I had to admit it was a great solution. Clearly my clients had a lot to teach me about marketing in the republic of Georgia.

And that's the whole fun of living abroad. You aren't doing things the same old way. You can't. Which means you're going to have to be open to new ways of thinking about *everything*.

Exploring new ways of approaching life can become addictive. "Abroad" is a very big place, and the possibilities are so intriguing that it's often hard to stop browsing and choose where you'd like to live. No matter how comfortably settled we are, Rich can never resist looking at real estate, and he automatically checks out housing prices wherever we travel so he can have the fun of imagining us living there.

"Listen to this," he said once, while reading a newspaper in the Himalayan kingdom of Bhutan. "You can get a three-bedroom house, with garden and toilet, for just four hundred thousand ngultrums. That's less than ten thousand dollars."

Reading the ad over his shoulder, I replied, "Yes, and it's conveniently located in downtown Wangdue Phodrang — which is where exactly?"

Rich had to admit that living in a small market town in central Bhutan might not give us the lifestyle we wanted, even with such bonus extras as garden and toilet.

Before our move to Seville, whenever we saw this kind of alluring real estate deal I would remind Rich of our agreement that we would never seriously consider living anywhere that we hadn't visited three times. We didn't want to make a move we'd repent at leisure. Like most Americans, I grew up on stories of immigrant forebears who left behind everyone and everything they knew forever in order to forge a new life in a new land. I find it immensely comforting to know that today you can try out places before you commit to them, and you can keep your ties to the old country in case things don't work out or just because you enjoy them both.

For me, things did work out. This is the story of why I moved to Seville and how I shaped a new life in a foreign country while maintaining a place for myself in my native land. My story will, I hope, provide you with some ideas about how *you* might experience living abroad in the world, if you ever decide to try it. It *is* possible — fun, even — to engage in a whole new culture, face up to its challenges, and build a life that's truly yours in a country that isn't. And we're lucky enough to live in an age where you can do all that without cutting your ties to your homeland.

This book describes my adventures and misadventures in Seville, but the lessons I've learned can be applied to any international move, whether it's to a bungalow in India, a flat in Moscow, or a *mieszkanie* in Warsaw. I've devoted chapters to the topics that people most often ask me about: learning a foreign language, finding housing, bringing along your beloved pet, making friends, adapting to unfamiliar eating and drinking customs, dealing with a very different health care system, and coping with the arrival of more houseguests than you could ever have imagined possible.

You'll learn about friends I made (some of whom appear here under other names, out of respect for their privacy) and mistakes I blundered into along the way. One of the great things about living abroad is that you have countless new ways to screw up, providing many valuable opportunities for honing your wits and your sense of the ridiculous.

We've all read articles about how to keep your brain's synapses firing by doing Sudoku, taking up knitting, or going bird watching, but frankly, I find life in a foreign country to be a far more interesting and effective way to stay sharp. The French writer Émile Zola once said, "If you ask me what I came into the world to do, I will tell you: I came to live out loud." And if you ask me, I will tell you there's nothing quite like going abroad to pump up the volume on your life.

Dancing in the Fountain is available from Amazon in Kindle and paperback.

ABOUT THE AUTHOR

My checkered past includes working as a journalist, editor, graphic designer, corporate communications director, and marketing consultant in Boston, California, and Cleveland. When my husband, Rich, took early retirement, we began volunteering as business consultants to struggling microenterprises in emerging and post-war nations. During our 36 years of marriage we've visited more than 60 countries, and when we discovered Seville in 2001, it kept calling us back. After several vacations there, each longer than the last, we decided to make it our home "for a year." We're still there and still in love with the city. We also spend time in the States, because America is something you have to stay in practice for, and we don't want to lose our touch.

When we reached our sixties, Rich and I began to wonder whether we could still have the kind of spontaneous travel adventures we'd enjoyed in our youth, so we set off to find out. We walked out of our Seville apartment and strolled to the train station with small, roll-aboard bags, a Eurail pass, and a railway map of Europe. With no reservations, no fixed time limit, and only a loose idea of an itinerary, we spent three months riding the rails, mostly through Eastern Europe. We had so much fun that a few years later we set off on a Baltics to Balkans journey and after that came our five-month Mediterranean Comfort Food Tour through thirteen countries.

The results of our journeys became two bestselling travel

memoirs, three guides, and a host of blog posts, interviews, and articles. My travel tips and adventure stories have appeared in *HuffPost, International Living Magazine, New York Daily News, Los Angeles Times*, and *Lonely Planet*.

Rich and I are now (gasp!) in our seventies, and we're still active travelers, when world conditions permit. Like everyone else, we're struggling to make sense of new entry requirements and adapt to the public health concerns of other countries (and our own). We hope someday to resume our longer journeys, but for now we're content to be in Seville, where I'm busy chronicling recent changes and figuring out how to navigate the new normal. You can read about my explorations and discoveries on my blog, EnjoyLivingAbroad.com. I hope you'll come take a look and stay for the ongoing conversation taking place in the comments section. The wisdom, humor, and insights of my readers continues to sustain and inspire me. I hope you'll become part of it.

CAFÉ
SOCIETY
PRESS

Café Society Press
Clearstead
E, 1100 Superior Ave, Suite 700
Cleveland, OH 44114 USA

enjoylivingabroad.com